To Swann,

My Greatest Friend

With all my Love

Prabodee

CONTENTS

AUTHOR'S NOTE

Dear Readers,

I have tried to write down my experiences with Bhagavan Sri Sathya Sai Baba exactly as they happened for you to read and hopefully share with me my feelings in finding the complete inner peace, and the reality of God.

I would like to thank Aunice Cambell for her tremendous patience in proof reading and her understanding thoughts whilst writing this book.

Thank you to all my friends in England, in India and the Bandboys for all their encouragement to put pen to paper.

I must also thank the Headmaster and staff at my school in England for their patience (and "comments") whilst I typed with one finger on the staff room computer!

This whole project could not have happened without Swami's loving Grace, and the collaboration of Mr. Anil Kumar, Mr. & Mrs. K.V. Krishnamurthy, Mr. Rao and Mr. Padmanaban......thank you all.

David Bailey

PREFACE

Strange are the ways of God. Bhagavan Baba's miracles are inscrutable. The experiences of the devotees of Sri Sathya Sai Baba are thrilling, exciting and fascinating. Sai Baba is a global phenomenon. His mission brings about a transformation in the life of any that comes to know Him, sees Him, talks to Him and feels Him. The Will of Sai is a silent revolution that calls for noticing divinity within, and its oneness all around. It is said that all roads lead to Rome, but today we can put it this way - all faiths lead to Parthi. People from all parts of the world of different religions, cultures, nationalities and spiritual pursuits find in "Swami" a fulfilment, and realization of their life long endeavours. Sai's Spiritual path is not one of negation or condemnation of any faith. In fact Sai's Spiritual way fosters, encourages and enriches every religion. It calls for practice and experience.

There are amongst Baba's devotees national leaders, Nobel Laureates, scientists, scholars, industrialists, top musicians, people from all walks of public life. He draws them in His own inimitable divine style towards Him, and fills their lives full of bliss and satisfaction. They see Him as a mentor, a guide directing their lives in every way, mundane and spiritual. Bhagavan Baba is the joy and glory of the world, and to be with Him is very heaven.

This book "A journey to love" written by David Bailey from England is an account of his experiences with Swami. The reader will definitely find it interesting throughout. Brother David had many mystic experiences before coming to Baba. He had once experienced astral travelling. Hailing from an orthodox Christian family, David has now become a most popular pianist, very much sought after throughout the world. How prophetic are the words told to him, "watch out for the age of 40, something tremendous will start to happen", by a palmist, that subsequently came true, as it was at this age of 40 he came to Baba!

It is only in the ground which is well ploughed and watered, that seeds grow. Similarly the field of human heart should be well tilled with detachment and renunciation where spiritual seeds germinate. At an early age David felt that accumulating money, making investments and using a lot of brain time doing this, were a total and utter waste of time, because in a flash the best laid plans may be smashed and the world may collapse around you. David was never of the view that art is for art's sake. He always felt within a purpose and a Divine mission behind his music. When a paralytic lady was healed and she regained all her faculties to his music therapy, he silently prayed to God to "help him to help others through music". His "other senses seemed to become stronger" so that he could look at a person and know their "problems" "family details" and so on. "All the moves... have happened unexpectedly" in his life.

Through Tony Budell he came to know about Sai Baba. He was amazed by the way Baba could "make a tough man like Tony change his life". He got vibhuthi, as he had wanted, in a miraculous way from Digby who said "He is telling me to give you some", evidently Swami had prompted him from within. Bhagavan is the indweller of everyone. This is experienced by David so he writes "if one asks a question seriously either in one's mind or aloud then along comes the answer as inspiration, or someone lends a book, or answers the question from their experiences with Swami". What an incredible miracle it is when he got 3000 pounds instantly, compensating for the loss sustained when he responded to His call "cancel all contracts from July and August"! His description of his first trip to India is so beautiful that you would feel you were there physically.

His first impression of Swami after "basking" in the divine Darshan of Swami is Unique. He says "I have come, I have found what I am looking for". He received energy from Baba which is "very beautiful, engulfing, enriching and can only be described as Love, bliss in the fullest meaning". It is fascinating to learn how Baba made him come back by arranging an air ticket. He feels "Swami will care for the individual in the most intimate way". Bhagavan's encompassing love is felt by David and he says "there are no words to express the feelings with which He enveloped me. He turned into the most loving being I had

ever seen. A sense of tremendous relief came over me because all the past seemed to fade away and I was given a clean slate again". Bhagavan assured him that his sins were "forgiven". Swami knows our innermost desires. David was granted a benedictory opportunity to play on the piano in the Divine presence of Swami. At that time he prayed "Swami, take our hands that we may play for you, take our voices that we may sing for you and take our bodies that we may dance for you." What is surrender beyond this!

Day by day life becomes sweeter and sweeter with Swami and there appears a new turn, a reformation, that David admits stopped his "monkey mind". One must not miss to read the incident of his name mysteriously appearing in the "confirmed list" for the 14th January flight back home. He suggests to the readers to pray to Swami: "I want to know You and be able to trust You... please help. Swami, I am sorry, please forgive me and be with me. Help me to feel Your presence with all Your love.. now.. Lord please...teach me to understand."

It will be of immense help to everyone of us if we pray at the beginning of every day and at the end of the day along the lines he suggests. Why not try? David's observation towards the conclusion is remarkable and needs a special mention. He says "Baba is here now to show us the way in the modern world and to guide each and every one of us towards a lifetime engulfed in the Love of God".

At the end David mentions some of his "favourite reflections" to muse over in a quiet minute or two. They constitute an excellent selection. They convey the essence of Sai message. "Truth is God. God is Truth. Live in Truth". "God is Love. Love is God. Live in Love." Quest for Truth is the noblest of all. Its publication is One's own duty. The present attempt by David is one such sacred duty. It is an eye-opener to those who are yet to know Baba. It is one of light and delight to all those who are devotees. I am sure this will receive the attention and appreciation of every reader and above all Bhagavan Baba's bounteous blessings.

Sai Ram.

Prasanthi Nilayam   K. ANIL KUMAR
1-3-96

Anil Kumar was Lecturer at the Andhra Christian College, Guntur (A.P.), in India and subsequently Director of the Sri Sathya Sai College at Whitefield, Bangalore. He was the State President of Sri Sathya Sai Organisations, Andhra Pradesh in India. He was sent by Bhagavan Baba as the guest speaker to Japan, Hong Kong and Thailand.

INTRODUCTION FROM THE EAST

Mr David Bailey is a renowned Piano Maestro who has now turned out to be an enlightened devotee of Sri Sathya Sai Baba. He has narrated in an illuminating way his experiences i.e., his search for Truth which brought him to India. In this book 'A journey to Love', the Author has given a vivid picture of his incredible and amazing journey which took him to the gates of heaven within a short span of two years. His achievements have been recognised by the Master of the Universe!

The author has dealt with the subject which is pure love classified under two categories. One part deals with divine love, the purest form of love and how it is transferred in the form of 'energy' from the Lord to the devotee, resulting in the transformation of the individual totally i.e., himself. The other part explains how, to his bewilderment, he found God - for whom he was searching - the one and the only one who loved and cared for each and every soul. This was the greatest achievement of his life and it was acknowledged by God himself! It was here that, being a Westerner, he could identify the greater Truth that Jesus and Sri Sathya Sai Baba are one.

The prophecy that he would achieve something fantastic at the age of 40, as told by the Scottish lady and the Gypsy while he was at school, blossomed to truth when he succeeded in his attempt to locate his Master in India who was none other than Sri Sathya Sai Baba. In his presence, the author could see, feel and experience the Sai Love being transferred to him in the form of energy. To quote in his own words, "Energy poured out of His hands in a kind of circular motion; it was not like an electrical energy, it was sheer love, so powerful, it was almost a glimpse of heaven. I burst into tears, I couldn't help it, the feeling was so beautiful."

The author has analysed and revealed to the western world, how Sri Sathya Sai Baba, the living God in human form, living in India, can bring about a complete transformation of an individual. Distance or religion is no bar, the author says, but the inner, earnest craving will work miracles. Each and every chapter reveals, in great detail, how his heart, head and hands responded to the divine message. He could delve into his teachings putting his heart and soul into the experience. The author calls Swami his Greatest Friend! He says that Swami is here to guide us to live out lives engulfed in the love of God. The reader can share something of the author's own experience of the highest truth, and what it is to begin to live with God every moment.

This illuminating book is an eye opener for all those who are in search of truth and those who want to get out of the misery and turmoil of this life and find solace in the love of God.

Sai Ram.

Mr. K. V. Krishnamurthy, now retired, was the Deputy Director General of the Geological survey of India.

INTRODUCTION FROM THE WEST

Do all Karma as actors in a play, keeping your identity separate and not attaching yourself too much to your role. Remember that the whole thing is just a play and the Lord has assigned to you a part; act well your part; there your duty ends He has designed the play and He enjoys it.

- Baba

When David called and asked me if I would write a preface to his book - the above sentence immediate came to my mind.

No one that I know act his part as well as David does, and no one plays his part so wholeheartedly as he does.

I met David first time during the World Music Festival in Prasanthi Nilayam in July 1995 where he represented England by talking and playing over the theme "Western Classical music and the three Gunas". The next day he gave a speech on the veranda, the only time I have ever seen anyone sitting on the Veranda on a tiny chair in a black morning dress. His talk to Swami and the assembled devotees was so full of joy and love that it melted all hearts.

Working with the organisation in Russia, I asked David if he would like to come and play and give a talk at the annual meeting in St. Petersburg for the

Russian speaking countries, where around 250 devotees from the huge area were assembled. Immediately David said "I will come" and gave us all an unforgettable evening. The best expression concerning that memorable evening was in a letter from the leader of the Sai Organisation in Bjelo Russia, Natalia Shamkova, who writes: "Our meeting with David, a musician, was a real present. His virtuosity, childish naturalness, humour, cheerfulness produced a real outburst in the heart of everybody present in the hall. Thank you, Thanks a lot. These are Love and care of Baba. Only He can do the impossible."

Due to Swami's grace, James Redmond from The Video Education Company was present, and this unforgettable evening has been recorded on Video. All these superlatives we now have in this book. David, I know that you will keep your humility in all lives to come and I am happy to be able to introduce this book from the hand of the "Clown of the Universe."

Sai Ram.

Steen Piculell

Copenhagen
February 1996

Steen Piculell is a Deputy Central Co-ordinator of Sri Sathya Organisations for the Russian speaking countries.

THE START OF MY JOURNEY

How many of us have wondered, even a little bit, as to whether there is a "God", or will I really die, and is it possible to live after I die in another place? Heaven? Paradise? the Spirit world? I'm sure you've heard of someone, who, whispering under their breath, said that a friend had been to a "psychic" who had told them all about their Aunt Jane being fine on the "other side". Equally, I'm sure you have met people who have said "Don't have anything to do with that.......it's the Devil!

My parents are Anglican, my father having been the church warden of the local church wherever we have lived. My grandparents were on one side Methodists and the other Congregationalists, so whichever set I stayed with as a child I could not escape "Church". I was a choirboy, and then as I grew into my early teens I learned to play the organ having already mastered the piano to a reasonable standard.

The whole of this time I could clearly relate to the stories of Jesus and would often daydream to being with Him as He walked and talked. I seemed to be able to accept His life story until the events at Easter, when something seemed very wrong and I did not inwardly accept that He died on the cross. I often wondered if I had been there at the time? The Church accepts that Jesus died on the cross, and reappeared after His death, but does not accept that this reappearance could happen to everyone.

One day the priest said that he had seen someone come and kneel beside him to say Evensong with him and then "disappeared", so he concluded he had seen a ghost! This was terrible.....but to my choirboy mind it was obvious, Jesus did it, so why couldn't we follow the same pattern? My interest was aroused in the subject, I wanted to know more.

When I stayed with my Methodist grandparents we would often go for long walks and Grandad took great pleasure in stopping and looking at the wild flowers and the intricate details of the flowers and the leaves. He often used to say "Look David, look carefully, the Person who made these cared so much for the detail to make these so beautiful, how much must He care for you? When we came across a superb view he would say "Look as far as the eye can see, God made this and imagine how many plants and insects there are there, He knows every one.

My Congregational grandfather was different; he had been to Canada in the twenties and the thought of this trip seemed to awaken in me a real interest in the traditions of the North American Indians. He had studied many different spiritual things and he started to explain what he had learned over the years. One evening with him I had my first experience; he was

2

sitting in his chair talking to me when, suddenly behind him, a Red Indian's head and full head dress appeared from nowhere. Grandad saw me looking sideways with a concerned look on my face, and asked me what I was looking at. "I can see a Red Indian standing next to you" I replied. "Oh good" he said, "Don't be concerned, that is my guide". He then went on to explain that the Church teaches us that we have a guardian angel as a child, but, in fact, we have a guardian who stays with us all our lives, and as we grow older some people can even sometimes see him [or her]. This made sense to me and, ever since then, I have occasionally seen or sensed someone very close to me or to the person I might be talking to..

Another experience I had when I was at school was with a lovely elderly Scottish lady who used to come and stay with my grandparents. I looked forward to her visits as we would sit and chat. She was able to tell me exactly what would happen to me, even to saving me doing my homework at home! Often she would say "Don't worry about your geography homework [for example] tonight, the geography master will be away tomorrow and you will be able to do it at school. The following day I would go to school, meet my chums who would moan about the homework, and when I said that I hadn't done it they were certain that I was going to get a detention........but, funnily enough, the master never turned up for the lesson!!!!

Before she died she told me something fantastic would happen when I reached the age of 40......

So, I had proof at an early age that in some way the future could be accurately foretold. I wanted to understand more and more. Behind all this world there had to be Someone who cared, but where, and who or what?

I discovered the work of Mother Theresa, and the love she showed in her work, but she was in India. There was a man by the name of Harry Edwards who I discovered had the gift of healing. He lived in England, and many people had been healed from all sorts of serious illnesses just by his touching.

Being an organist I was in great demand, and on a Sunday I would play for at least 5 services in different churches as there was a shortage of organists. The churches changed the times of their services so that I could race from one to the next. There were Anglican, Baptist, Methodist, and even occasionally a "Spiritualist Church". The first time I played there, I went with some trepidation as I had been warned to "Keep clear of them - they call up the dead!" How wrong were these friends of mine who had warned me. From a musicians' point of view, yes, the hymns were a bit reminiscent of Victoriana and slushy poetry, but these churches, as I was to quickly discover,

4

often had a lovely feel to them. The people who took the services were very often sincere people who had a natural gift of being able to see people we couldn't see and to hear them speak.

Didn't Jesus do this?

How could this be wrong when the messages given to the people in the church were so personal about a husband, mother, father, each one conveying love and giving proof that they knew what was going on in their individual lives. I thought for a bit.....yes, it must be mind reading, or somehow the people themselves giving clues as they replied.

In the meantime my schoolwork had to continue, and my father, being as part of his responsibilities, careers officer, continually reminded me that to get a place on a graduate course I must get at least two good "A" levels......so work hard!!

Quietly, my Scottish lady told me that I was not to worry, everything was "planned", just keep playing the piano. I went for my audition for the graduate course at Trinity College of Music....as soon as I had played I was sent to the principal of the college, who offered me an *unconditional* place....no "A" levels required. When I returned home with the news, needless to say my father did not believe me......until the letter arrived confirming the very rare situation........ my lady was right again!

5

Having got my degree, I had an opportunity to produce my first cassette as a professional pianist, and somebody that I had worked with, wanted to back me and promote my career. We had agreed to sign contracts in the presence of his solicitor two weeks later. Shortly afterwards I was walking round a Fun Fair which had come into town and saw a fortune teller's caravan, so I plucked up courage and went in. The gypsy said to me "Young man you should be on the stage playing the piano [yes, exactly what I wanted to do I thought], but you must not sign up with the wrong person. You will know the wrong person because he will be made a Lord.......DO NOT SIGN WITH HIM!" She was very emphatic. She then said a few things about the family etc., which were accurate, but not outstanding, so I thanked her and wandered off wondering what she was talking about because my contact was a business man and, as far as I knew, was not in that league. So I rather dismissed the whole incident.

I went down for the appointment 2 weeks later, 10 a.m. as agreed. There were a lot of cars at his house, and I went in to find all his friends there drinking champagne ———— I said that I thought this was a bit of a grand celebration just for me to sign the contract. "No", he said, " I've inherited a Lordship, I'm now Lord......" I went hot and cold and the words of the gypsy rang in my ears, so I plucked up courage and refused to sign. Circumstances arose shortly afterwards which showed I would have had a major disaster if I had signed.

How had she known? There must be something there that we can tap into, rather like tuning in on a radio when looking for a particular wavelength.

In the meantime, I had built up a piano business and several music shops which brought me about 5 years of chasing money, overdrafts and travelling round Europe. There was a tremendous excitement in "doing deals", but the trouble was that once a deal had been struck it all faded away, and one scrambled for the next one. Luckily, as I now realise, lots of my foreign contacts went bankrupt, and like a pack of cards took all my business too. By the grace of God [to use the expression, but I now know that this was part of the plan] I lost everything, house, car, all those carefully planned policies, yet was never declared bankrupt personally. I had one thing left, an old caravan in which for a few months I lived in England in a tiny copse alone. No, I wasn't frightened, bored or bitter, somehow I knew I had to stop and think. Watching the sun rise through the trees, I soon learnt that the old saying "Red sky at night shepherds' delight, Red sky in the morning shepherds' warning" meant for me" make sure the water cans are full or I'll get wet later on!"

During these years I had been stopped by at least a dozen people in the street, some were the old gypsies who said "10p for a bunch of heather —— you'll travel a lot, don't worry, you should be on the stage, or you are a musician." They were always encouraging and had some close connection with my situation.

I went to see an expert on palmistry, who worked closely with the police. After having great difficulty in taking prints from my hands,he explained how the different lines on the hand represented different periods of my life, health, what I had achieved and what I could achieve. They showed up the collapse of my business, not being married, WATCH OUT FOR THE AGE OF 40, SOMETHING TREMENDOUS WILL START TO HAPPEN........ and this was for the second time .....what could it be?

I had the chance to meet lots of "clairvoyants", some good , some not. My thoughts were that if a dead person was standing next to the clairvoyant, and for example it was my grandfather, he would know everything about himself, and if I asked him where he had lived here on earth he would be able to tell me; there was no need for bluff or guesswork. If it was true it was accurate. When I found mediums that were accurate, the evidence was stunning, so I was accepting the fact that there is life in some form after this one [Jesus has continued to live!].

8

I also met many people who were healers in their own way, some who just touched the sick person, some by putting crystals on them, often with quiet background music gently playing. There are of course the various interdenominational church services for healing. Some people claim you must believe. Some say that it doesn't matter whether you believe in it. Some say that even if you don't know that you are being given healing, it will work.

I was searching for the truth. So many of these people went so far, then said "I believe that......" I wanted to KNOW. Jesus proved what He did, so why can't this be proved.

Some friends wanted me to try yoga, transcendental meditation, astral travel, get a guru, all of which meant a great deal to them, but which to me were only part of a jigsaw puzzle, pieces, and I was desperate to find the picture and not get stuck on just one of the pieces. I did have one odd experience with astral travelling. I was at my house alone, when I suddenly thought about my very close friends in Palermo in Sicily. I thought to myself; I wondered if it really is possible to go somewhere without transport. The next second I had arrived in my friend's kitchen! Maria the wife was cooking, and their next door neighbour had called in very distressed, and was talking to the father of the family. After what seemed to be a few minutes Maria looked up, and was about to say "David!" when I was suddenly back at my house in England again. The next morning I telephoned, and the father answered, amazed that I was still alive, because they had seen me the previous evening in their kitchen and feared that I had died and had appeared as a ghost. They confirmed that their next door neighbour had been there, and very upset, and Maria had turned round from her cooking and seen me for a moment and then I had disappeared. It was a fascinating experience, I felt nothing, only here one minute and in Palermo the next at a thought......??

This period of my life had certainly taught me one thing and it was that to chase money, accumulate money for money's sake, make investments and use a lot of brain time doing this were a total and utter waste of time, because in a flash the best laid plans can be smashed, and the world seems to collapse around you........except for that yearning feeling that God DOES exist and is always there. He can't be bought or sold. All the people I had met had their own particular directional pointers for me, so follow......but where to?

I had my caravan towed over to France, to a little village on the coast just outside Calais called Wissant. I already loved France and had played the piano there so I found it easy to find places in which to play. I stayed there for nine months unwinding from the previous five years hard work looking for clues as to which way I should go in the future. One night I was sitting playing the piano when an elderly lady came up to me, and in English said "Young man, you should be on stage with your own show called My Piano and Me". I returned to England at the end of their summer season and was offered four shows in Ilfracombe, North Devon. These sold out, and a further nine successful shows promoted the start of my touring round England with my own show.

Again following my instinct, hunting for what I should be doing, the signs were to entertain people, especially older folk, making them happy. Someone suggested that by playing the tunes that the older people remember, they were taken back to when they were young, before they had all their problems, angina, arthritis, rheumatism, and so on, and that if they did this successfully then, after the concert, their conditions may have improved or even disappeared ....an interesting thought.

My next "lesson" was at Paignton. We had an afternoon show, and the theatre was full of senior citizens. At the interval a man on the front row seemed to be raving over the show, jumping up and down and applauding. At the end of every show I always go into the foyer to say goodbye to the audience personally. This afternoon the only way to the foyer was to go down some steps off the front of the stage. As I did so, this man jumped up and put his

11

arms around my neck hugging me, saying "Thankyou, Thankyou!" To be honest, I thought at the time his behaviour rather bizarre, and I was embarrassed. Eventually I escaped and went to the foyer, only to be met by my stage manager, Roger, who told me that I must go back to this man. I didn't want to, but reading the look in Roger's eyes I had to go back, so I did. The man explained that two months previously his wife had had a severe stroke leaving her whole body paralysed ,so he had brought her in a wheelchair. At the end of the first half he had noticed her left foot tapping to the music, and then he said "Look, she is standing over there talking to her friends and she has regained all her faculties." What had happened? Was it the show? The music? Was it psychological? What could not be denied was that something marvellous had happened for that lady. I wondered.....yes please, I thought, if I can help people like that, please "God" help me to do so.

My playing took me through France and several times down to Palermo in Sicily. Whenever I was in Palermo my "other senses" seem to become much stronger. I could look at a person and immediately, without thinking at all, know when they would get married, their problems, family details and so on. I couldn't understand why this happened in Palermo and not at home in England. My friends in Palermo insisted that I visit a chapel in the mountains at the back of Palermo, dedicated to Santa Rosalia, the patron saint of Palermo. This, apparently, was where if you made a wish it would come true. Well, in for a penny in for a pound [or should I say lire] I went to this beautiful chapel high in the mountains above Palermo. The chapel itself is an old cave in the side of the mountain. I walked in, and immediately sensed a very beautiful atmosphere. Suddenly the little voice in my head started talking to me, "You are here now, kneel quietly and listen, you do have a wish, so think and make it seriously, we are listening." I made my wish, and it has and is coming true with my current experiences with Sai Baba. I must have spent many many hours sitting up there "listening" in the chapel.

One Tuesday evening in February 1991, the telephone rang at home. It was a good friend from some 10 years previously who had taught geography at a preparatory school where I had been Director of Music before the school had closed. He was now teaching at one of the leading preparatory schools in England and they had got a problem; their Music master had been taken ill in the middle of a production of Joseph and his Amazing Technicolour Dreamcoat. Could I start the next day, and take over for the rest of the term? As it was February my own shows were quiet as most of the theatres still had pantomimes running, so I agreed to stand in. Again a little lesson. All the moves I have had to make in my life have all happened completely Unexpectedly to me. I didn't apply for this position which is one of the most prestigious jobs in this field, but was given it.

This gave me not only more financial security, but also a lot of time to continue to perform around the country. I had time to think. I met Michael Bentine, and read his book called Doors of the Mind. This explained a great deal of my feelings and things I had experienced, and seemed to set me on my spiritual path with increased determination to find .... whatever it was I was looking for.

I saw the work of the pendulum and the way some people can use it to find things, or to tell right from wrong. Water diviners are fascinating to watch in the way twigs, or bent coat hangers, bounce up and down over water. Some friends had got a table to move by itself and played around [foolishly in my opinion] with the Ouiji board with the glass flying round the table. Think what you will, right or wrong, the fact is that the glass moved. I found healers who could cure people, yet six months later they were often back in their original condition.......why didn't it last?

The more I saw, heard and learnt showed me that there was an energy that could be tapped into in many different ways to cause things to happen. It also seemed that this could be used for good or, unfortunately, for bad. So what made the great teachers, especially Jesus, different? What did they add to this energy that we were, or were not missing? So many of the abilities I had found people possessed were as natural to the person practising them as playing the

14

piano was to me. I didn't have to think where middle C was on the piano, or how the music was written, my eyes saw the written music and my fingers played it. Was it a "Gift" or my profession? Whatever you call it, it happens naturally without thought. The water diviner does not think "sticks bounce, sticks bounce", he just holds them and off they go, he cannot help it, it just happens.

Did Jesus care for the world and His disciples? Yes. So did He use this energy in a caring way, in fact in a loving way (at the time I wanted to say this, but was afraid of Victorian sentimentality coming out)?

Then my thoughts recalled the hell, fire and damnation sermons I had heard at church and remembered the scenes of what seemed to be mass hysteria at some of the religious rallies. Where was the LOVE, not the word, but the REALITY of LOVE.

I wanted the world to be full of it. Imagine how fantastic it would be if everyone cared about everyone else? It must be possible........what about this new Aquarian age that other friends talked about....yes..... the concept was possible, mathematically and astrologically it must happen, but to my mind without that love, it would only be a change of energy into a new period. If we added that LOVE, what could then happen?

Ah well, back to school routines, choose another hymn for chapel, more reports, sort out new programmes for the concerts, tax and insure the car. The so called "real" world called again and the search goes on!

A JOURNEY TO LOVE

The Wednesday after Easter 1994 I was walking nearby school, in Broadstairs, when I saw a notice that said there was to be an evening about Sai Baba at a small hall called the Star of the East, about half a mile from school. To this day I do not know why I went to that evening, apart from now understanding that Swami (another name for Sai Baba) had planned my invitation.

This particular night the speaker was Tony Budell, who told us of his interesting experiences. The thing that impressed me more than anything was the fact that he had, through, as he said, trusting Sai Baba, given up his job as a porter in Canterbury Hospital and started, with the help of a few friends, a new Charity which took relief supplies to Bosnia and Croatia every month. The previous Christmas Swami had told him to take 100 lorries to Bosnia! This I remembered seeing on television, and the whole concept seemed admirable, and rather rare in this day and age. This man, Sai Baba, must have had something very convincing and genuine to make a tough man like Tony change his life.

Tony then went on to say that Swami would produce gold, silver rings, watches etc, from his hands, let alone the very special vibhuti. This is a kind of "sacred" ash which is often used for medicinal purposes.

17

This, at the time, seemed a great disappointment to me......why did the person who Tony referred to as God on earth, manifest as man, need to do tricks?

I went home very thoughtful!

The next night I had a show at the Theatre Royal at Portsmouth. After the show, back at the hotel, I lay in bed thinking again over the previous evening. "Well", I thought to myself, "If this so called vibhuti exists, I want to see some." Since childhood I have, from time to time, had a little voice which seems to speak into my ear. That night, as soon as I had thought this about the vibhuti, I heard "Ok, but there's no need to go to India to see some." I did not understand how this could be possible, so I went to sleep.

The next morning a good friend had organised me to go and see a man called Digby Curtis, who was interested in pyramids and had built one in his back garden. So we travelled over to the Isle of Wight, out into the country at the back of Freshwater where there was a lovely cottage with a well cared for garden— everything homegrown! We went in and chatted for a couple of hours about Egypt, the pyramids and, eventually, Digby suggested that we went and sat inside the one he had built at the bottom of his garden. It was quite large and about a dozen people could get inside to sit and meditate if they wished. As he opened the "door", I spotted a photo on the floor of Sai Baba, so I said "Oh, Sai Baba". "Yes", he said, "Do you know of him?" "Well, sort of " I said. After we'd chatted some more after he said "David, I want to give you something". He reached behind the picture and produced a packet of something that looked like grey ash. "This is vibhuti," he said, "Not from Swami's hands, but blessed by him, and I want to give it to you." I was stunned . I remembered my little voice....you don't have to go to India to get some vibhuti —but I wanted some vibhuti from His hands, so only 8 out of 10. After another two or three minutes I noticed a tear in Digby's eyes, and he said to me "David, one day you will understand, but Swami is standing here now telling me to give you something special, because last year we were in India with Him, and He granted us an interview, and materialized some vibhuti for us, which we have kept. He is telling me to give you some!"

I'm afraid I cried too, with the intense emotion I felt. Now it had to be 10/10. I had my vibhuti from Him within hours of His promise.

I wanted to understand more and more about this "man". Digby was kind, and patiently explained what he knew. The time came to leave and, just as I was going, Digby said "Hang on a moment, I've got something else". He gave me a beautiful photo of

Swami. I went hot and cold because nobody knew that one of my favourite places for quietness is the chapel of Santa Rosalia in the mountains at the back of Palermo in Sicily, and this photo was as if Swami was standing outside this chapel with the mountains falling away behind him .....another tear.

I returned home to Broadstairs <u>very</u> thoughtful. Who had I found? Was He the person I have been searching for, or is He another crazy religious freak? I must know more. Every day during the following week I met somebody who knew about Swami. I was lent a couple of books, and one day I thought I would like, somehow, to get a photo of Swami into the music room. Just as I was leaving a friend's house she said, "David, have you got a Swami calender?"......the very thing for the music room, an innocent calender that just happened to have Swami's face on it! So, up on my cupboard door it went. Then I was given a small photo of Swami for my wallet. I was very pleased to have Him in my pocket all the time now.

Now came my first lesson. I had a 'phone call from a friend who, over the past few years had been made bankrupt, and whose life was very difficult. He asked me to go round to his house to have a chat with his wife and himself. We got talking about many things and eventually started talking about Swami. He was very interested, and wanted to hear all that I knew......my little voice said "Give him the photo".........."No it's mine" I thought. It is precious to me, it was given to me for my wallet, so I shall keep it........ "Give it to him"... "NO".

As I continued talking, so in my head the voice kept saying "Give him the photo". However I didn't, and the evening ended with my friends of many years very emotional. I went to my car and the husband came to see me off. He was in tears. I wound down my window and he said "Goodbye", then added "David, please, have you got a photo of Swami that I could have?"

I felt sick. How could I have been so thoughtless and selfish when my little voice had told me to give him the photo. After all I had been given. I gave it to him with love and drove away; but I stopped round the corner and cried for half an hour, ashamed. How could I have been so self-centred? Well, I had been, and this was the first of many lessons I was to learn.

As time went past, the more I learnt that if one asked a question seriously, either in one's mind or actually spoken when alone, the answer came either as "inspiration", or someone would lend a book or answer the question from their experiences with Swami.

I was invited to go to a Sai Baba day on the following Bank Holiday. I went with great reservation, slightly fearing a group of aged "Flower-Power hippies" with long hair, wearing extraordinary clothes and freaking out. I'm sure the organisers of the day would still be laughing if they had known my inner thoughts whilst driving the 100 miles to the venue. I arrived—well how wrong could one be! These were very nice people from all walks of life and we had a remarkable day, listening to peoples' fascinating experiences with Swami. In fact, this day convinced me that Swami was a very, very lovely man. I decided to follow His work seriously. Suddenly, my little voice said "Cancel all contracts for July and August." What! I thought. I had already several dates, publicity ordered and contracts signed. "Cancel them!" it came again. So I picked up the 'phone and cancelled the contracts. Then I went hot and cold because by cancelling them I was still incurring the publicity expense and the broken contract clause. This was going to cost some £3,000 which I had not got—— Swami help! I still had no thoughts whatsoever about going to India. Within twenty minutes of making the decision to cancel the telephone rang, and I was asked to do some business relating to arrangements made some eight years previously that was to generate £3,000 instantly!

The term went on and I was lent some very interesting videos, and on one of the videos there was an Indian man whose face stuck in my mind. His eyes seemed to tell me that he had found something very

22

special and that he had found complete contentment. I thought no more about him, yet his face stayed with me.

Straight after the end of term I decided to spend a few days on the Isle of Wight, and, since I loved France, I would then take my van and piano for a six week jaunt down to the south west of France.

Whilst on the Isle of Wight, I was taken to another friend's house to see the video of the new Super Speciality Hospital that Swami had built at Puttaparthi. A fantastic video....try to see it if you can.....as it explains every aspect of this large hospital built for anyone in the world to use free of charge. After watching this they asked me to play for a singer at their own Sai Baba day to be held on the island in September. I readily agreed, and booked the date in my diary. Digby said that Renu, the singer, was recording a cassette in Spain, dedicated to the work of Swami. We returned to Digby's house and the telephone rang. It was Renu! Coincidence? I don't think so! I was able to speak to her about September and what she wanted to sing. I said that I understood that she was in Spain. "No" she said, "I'm recording in Andorra at the end of August". "Great", I said, "I shall be in the south of France then, perhaps I can come and help you?" "Yes" she said, "I can't do it before because in ten days I am taking a party to India for three weeks to see Swami." Then she paused, and said "David, there is one space left on the trip: Would you like to come?" Once again I went hot and cold. Was this temptation, coincidence, or what? I thought about it for a couple of hours and rang her back saying that I would go. I now had to organise a passport, visa, injections, etc. However, if I was meant to go, it would work itself out.

Within me I wanted proof that it was right to go, because I had developed a great respect for Swami. Either way, if He was" just" a very great man or, in fact, a very Holy man as some people were quietly pointing out to me then, if I was to go , I must not waste His time and energy by going on a tourist trip! So I went out into the garden and I talked to Him as though He was next to me, and I explained how I felt and, if He was able to perform marvellous things at a distance, please would He prove to me in no uncertain terms that He wanted me to go.

I returned home next day, rather dreading telling my parents that I was going to India to see Sai Baba. I feared they would think that their son had lost his senses completely and was on the trail of some weird guru (how far from the truth)! However, my parents accepted the idea without any explanations required. Something was not quite right! Then mother owned up and said that a friend of ours, who sings in the local Church choir, had telephoned to say that, when she was quietly having a cup of tea at home, "something" had come to her and told her to ring David's parents to tell them that he was coming home with news of a long journey he was going to make. This journey was to do with the Church, but not the established Church as we know it, but the church of the future. He has a job to do so please let him go. Well, they were not expecting me back then, so when I turned up a few minutes later with this news they felt that they could only go along with it. This was quite good proof, but not good enough for me, so I went to see my grandmother who was 94 years old, and who for the previous couple of years had not known me, or anyone else, as unfortunately her mind had become total confusion,

I arrived and the sister at the nursing home went into her room and said " Hello Googie, (our pet name for her) we've a lovely visitor for you this afternoon." "Yes" she said,"That will be my David. He's going to India you know." What did she say? The sister came out of the room, indicating I could go in, and giving me a look as if to say "Make head or tail of that!" Little did she know. I went in, and Googie looked at me and said "Hello David, I'm so pleased to see you, because you are going to India to see Sai Baba aren't you?" I couldn't believe my ears. There was no way she could have known. My parents had not been in to see her, and I was the only one who knew I would be going to India. Grandma then reverted back in to her normal conversation of "The men climbing up the wall" or "Take the dog out of the fireplace"......total rubbish. Here was <u>my</u> proof I wanted. I had to go to India.

This meant a full passport, as all foreign travel so far in my life had been limited to Europe which could be done on a year's passport and to get a10 year passport, I needed my birth certificate, which I had lost, and so I had to chase around the country to get a copy from the registrar in the town where I was born. Then back up to the Passport office in Peterborough in person as there was no time to risk the post. So with injections done, visa obtained in London and my case packed with malaria tablets, loo rolls, hot chocolate, horlicks, a supply of snack bars, towel and sandels (I had been told you could buy the rest in Bangalore), we met at Heathrow. We flew out by Gulf airlines to Bombay, via Abu Dhabi and Muscat. We changed planes for the internal flight to Bangalore. Here we arrived quite late in the evening and were taken by taxi to our hotel. The taxi ride was a real introduction to India, the car itself was a real old banger, bald tyres, and the driver had the habit of turning off the headlights, despite the darkness, and continually sounding the horn. What a din! Then we realised that you can drive as you wish with no apparent rules of the road! Well, at least we were in the back seat!

We arrived at the hotel and we agreed to share rooms. There were four men and twelve women and a child in our group. The hotel had not kept enough rooms for us, so they had to bring extra mattresses into each room to make more beds. I had already owned up to being a hearty snorer (and have been banned from at least one hotel in England!), so they put my bed into the bathroom!

The next day, we breakfasted at the hotel with lovely fresh pineapple juice, toast and coffee. Really delicious, and all for about 50p. Then we all went into Bangalore to change some money, and we saw in daylight the driving we had experienced the night before. Well, I thought, they know what they are doing, I hope! The Indians have an incredible system (?) of driving, dodging the bumps, potholes, monkeys and, of course, the cow, being a sacred animal, is allowed to go whererever it wants and cause chaos in city traffic!

We tried several banks before we found one that would change our money. Then off to get some light suits to wear. We went to Commercial street, the most incredible shopping street I have seen......you can buy anything there, so cheaply. Here we came across the situation that I know bothers a lot of people because there were beggars everywhere. A lot of them had terrible handicaps.....missing limbs etc, really quite horrible to see. In England poor people exist, but the state looks after them in every way. Here they seemed to be left to their own devices, although we had been warned that many of them made a good business out of the foreigner who felt sorry for them. Remembering that 10 rupees to them was a day's money (20p), it was easy for us to give, say, a 50 or 100 rupee note (which was £1 or £2) which to us was nothing, but to them two or three times a day meant wealth.

Now the afternoon had come, and we decided to go to Whitefield, which is a few kilometres outside Bangalore, to see Swami for the first time.In comparison to travelling from the airport to the hotel this was a marathon journey.......would the taxi make it we wondered?

We arrived and the men and women had to separate to go and sit in their respective lines, waiting to go in. We didn't have to wait long, and soon we were sitting in the covered area where Swami was to come out and walk around a set route amongst the people gathered, to give them His blessing and collect some of their letters. This I discovered was called "Darshan". This particular afternoon, as it turned out, He just came and sat on a rather lovely chair at the front, whilst the college boys (about 300 of them) led the singing of Bhajans, which in an odd sort of way are used in the same way as our hymns. One person sings a line, and then everyone repeats it, often with everyone clapping along at the same time. I was at the end of a row, and everyone was sitting on the cushions crosslegged. Well I am quite a large chap, and to sit crosslegged was near impossible, and any attempt to do so was very very uncomfortable. So I stretched my left leg out straight. The next minute one of the "helpers" (sevadals as I discovered they were called) came and sat down beside me. He tapped my leg and said "Can you please sit properly". I turned to him, about to explain, when he realised it must have been my first visit and said "I'm sorry, you are a Westerner, please sit comfortably". I looked at his face and was dumbfounded. It was the face of the man I had seen on the video in England, the face that I remembered because I felt he had found something special, and here he was sitting next to me. Everyone was silent, a rather unusual, but very comforting, feeling with several thousand people sitting still and quiet. This mean't that I couldn't speak to him, then the Bhajans started. "Oh no!", I thought, "I can't stand this sound", but after a while I got used to them, and now in fact I enjoy them very much.

The moment came when Swami appeared and walked to his chair and sat down, looking at the crowd of some 7,000 people in front of him. I looked at Him, and I wondered why I had travelled thousands of miles to see Him.......He was just a man. I had played for many big showbusiness stars in England, so I knew what the feeling was to be in the presence of a "personality" and the hysteria it can produce in the public. This situation was not having this effect on me. Why? What is it? I wondered. Then suddenly something hit me in the chest, like a burst of energy that had a beautiful feeling about it. The energy travelled up my throat and hit my eyes with intense emotion. I flowed with tears. I felt a complete fool because my mind was saying "stop it", yet my inner-most-self, or soul as you might call it, was saying "I've come home, I've found what I'm looking for!" I took a sideways look at my three friends, afraid that they were laughing at me, at my age in floods of tears. Then I saw that they were in the same condition...tears pouring down their faces, having similar experiences. I then realised that this energy was not coming from the man, it seemed to be coming through Him and my body knew, not just my mind, that this was an experience of, to use the word, "God". The energy was very very beautiful, engulfing, enriching, and can only be described as Love, Bliss in the fullest meaning. I was fascinated, excited, and tried to open every pore in my body to receive it.

One of the pieces of advice I had been given was to remain quiet for 15 minutes after Swami had gone, to allow this energy He had given to be absorbed. To my— to be honest— horror, after He had gone most of the people got up, chatted and wandered off. I could not believe my ears, because these last few minutes for me had been very beautiful, as though one had been left under a hairdryer blowing only energy! So, if you do ever go to see Him, ignore everyone else who moves and chats, stay silent....I promise you it will be lovely.

That night we returned to the hotel in Bangalore and had a nice meal so cheaply it seemed impossible. Again I slept in the bathroom! Up the next morning to take the taxi at 4a.m. to Whitefield again for the morning Darshan at 6.45a.m. We had been given permission to go into the front section where a lot of the doctors, teachers and regular visitors go. This meant that, thank goodness (for me!), we didn't have to sit waiting in the lines, as our line was allowed to stand. We eventually went in and sat down. I positioned myself on the end of a line again and, lo and behold, the same man came and sat beside me. Swami came out and walked round this time....the same energy came with Him, it was fantastic. Afterwards, having waited the 15 minutes, I went to find the man who had sat next to me. He was just coming out of the bookshop. I went up to him, and said "Hallo, or should I say Sai Ram?" This is the expression that everyone uses. It seems to cover everything, hello, goodbye, excuse me, etc. "I am David, and I come from England. I have seen your face on a video in England, and I remember it clearly. Since you have now sat beside me, I feel I must introduce myself." He could not believe he was on a video, but said if I had got half an hour to spare he would like to talk to me.

Whilst waiting for Darshan, I had asked Swami mentally what I should be thinking whilst I was there. Over the past few months I had been able to ask a question and very soon afterwards I would get an answer in my mind. Today, I had no reply and I was a bit puzzled.

This Indian gentleman gave me his card "K.V. Krishnamurthy". He said, "I would like to talk to you about something you need to think about whilst you are here!" So the answer was coming this way. "David, who are you? What are you doing? Where do you come from and where are you going?"

"Easy", I thought, "I'm David Bailey, pianist, Director of Music, trying to help others in my own way. I come from England and I am searching for my future."

"No, no, no," he said kindly, "You are David from the family of Bailey in this life. You are God. God is in everyone you come from, and you return to God. Your thoughts are for the material world. You are here to develop spiritually." So the conversation went on.

I decided to ask Swami to do one thing for me. Please, when I had got my thoughts along the correct lines, would He please just look me in the eyes. That's all. Then, I would be sure that I was on the right lines.

The next Darshan we were nearer again to Him. He looked at everybody along my line until he got to me. His eyes went over my head and on to the next person. I talked again with my new friend who I also discovered had been with Swami for 27 years, so he had much to tell me.

He asked me to meet him the next day after Darshan to have a chat with another David from America. The next morning came, and we were standing out at the front in amongst about 60 men, and my friend came up to me and said "So you've found David then". "No", I said, "I don't know David". "You are standing next to him, touching his arm in line!" Coincidence? We got chatting and, as we sat down, he said that he had a sore throat. So I said "Why don't you ask Swami for something to help your throat?" "Ok" he said, and he sent a mental thought to Swami.

This morning Swami came down our line, and I had seen a man empty a large packet of boiled sweets on to a tray some ten yards away. All these sweets had clear wrappers. Swami went to him and blessed the sweets and, as is His custom, He picked up a handful and threw them into the air. Two went straight across me and landed at David's feet. He picked them up and whispered to me to look.......they were two Vicks (throat lozenges) ! Swami walked past, looking around but not into my eyes.

I thought again, I could not help thinking, "I am David, I play the piano. I want to work for God". What was wrong with that? So I wrote a letter to Swami from my heart. The next Darshan, Swami came past, took my letter, but still didn't look at me.

Renu, in the meantime, had organised a bungalow for us to stay in about half a mile away on a small estate where people can stay whilst visiting Swami. It was in a filthy state, so we all mucked in, washing, scrubbing, cleaning everything......floors, walls and ceilings. Luckily we were offered another bungalow after one night of cramming seventeen people into three rooms and the kitchen! This second one had two continental toilets, a hot shower (luxury!) and even a box room for me to snore in to my hearts content by myself. We started talking about our different experiences and soon realised that each one of us was looking for, or wanting, something different from the next. Some seemed to want to know about their practical everyday life, a change of job, or personal problem. Others were just "onlookers" and others, like me, were there on a spiritual "quest".

Each Darshan we sat nearer and nearer to Swami yet, as He walked past, He continued to look around me, not into my eyes as I asked, so I had still got it wrong. Again I wrote to Him from my heart and as He came past the next Darshan He took the letter, still not looking at me. Every day I drew closer to my new friend Krishnamurthy. He would explain more and more of Swami's teachings until, one day, I thought I had cracked it. I waited eagerly for Swami's Darshan. Yes, He was coming down our line......here He comes....and He's looking our way. He got in front of me and not only did He look away, He turned His back on me. Wrong again! I was very disappointed inside. However, I started to think again. I have my life, my job, my concerts, family, and Swami wants you to go back to your job etc., and put His love and teachings into your daily life. I had sorted this out, so there must be more. Who am I? Who or what is God? It is not Swami the man, that is only the form that we as humans can understand, because, if He appeared as a whirlwind or fire or some unknown energy, we would be frightened and could not relate to Him. So I thought on.

Next day, Swami came close, closer and then stood in front of me, and, yes, looked me straight in the eyes. I've really cracked it now, I thought, at least the first tiny step. Those eyes! How deep, beautifully soft and full of love, a fantastic moment never to be forgotten. If you ever get the chance grab it, and look as long as you can, and you will understand the beauty of this moment.

The next Darshan, He came down our line again, and this time I held out my Swami medallion and chain for Him, hopefully, to bless. He smiled and put His right hand on mine, giving me a long look again. I felt on top of the world.

The following day Krishnamurthy invited me back to his home for lunch and to talk. It was a lovely time and his son offered to take me to a concert of classical Hindu music, but, when I discovered it was the same time as Darshan, I declined, and we returned to Whitefield on the family scooter. I must have been an awful passenger, perched on the back! The roads were terrible and I was covered in dust by the time we arrived; Swami was just coming out for Darshan and again He made directly for our line. He walked past then, turning back, looked at me and said, "Where do you come from?" "U.K. Swami, there are seventeen of us" I replied. He came to me and put His hand, palm downwards, about eighteen inches from my eyes and waved it in a circular motion. Suddenly ash fell from the palm of His hand. This was the vibhuti, and was something I had wanted to see happen . I cupped my hands and caught it as it fell. Then He pointed his thumb at me and vibhuti seemed to come out of the end of his finger, which He then swiped vertically on my forehead between my eyes. What an incredible feeling, the energy transfer was terrific. I was now shaking like a jelly, not knowing where I was or what was happening. A good friend on the trip with us was Rakesh, a young accountant, who was sitting beside me. Rakesh grabbed my trembling hands, and tipped the vibhuti on to a piece of paper so that it was saved. The colour of the ash this time was white.

Why did He do that to me? This was serious. I hoped it was true that He had something for me to do to help His work.

The next day, the group went to see the Super Speciality, Hospital at Puttaparthi. This was some three and a half hours drive away and is Swami's home village, at which there is a huge ashram, a general hospital, school, college, university, and this incredible new huge hospital, the second largest in Asia. I was too "spaced out" to go, I just wanted to think and listen by myself.

Looking back over this two week period, I realised the tremendous change in my emotional state. In the first place it had been, for several days, the release, the floods of tears as the past seemed to be let go, almost an inner cleansing. This turned to joy and feelings of fulfilment, exhilaration and sheer "bliss". Often, I would have the feeling of walking on air and the real world, as I knew it before this trip, seemed an illusion, almost a farce in which everyone had a role to play. Now I realised there was far more to this world than I had ever previously dreamt of. So let's begin the finding out!

Our last two or three days were lovely. We heard Swami deliver a lecture. The translater was Mr Anil Kumar, then the Director of the College at Whitefield, who, to our surprise and joy came to our little bungalow that evening and gave our group a very interesting hours talk. It was again exhilarating to meet someone who worked so closely with Swami, and to experience that energy and love through this lovely man.

I was happy within myself. I had now found the pathway I had been searching for. Swami had come very close every time. He blessed some sweets that I had taken and then, on the last day, I was able to ask him. "Swami, this is our last Darshan, please may we go home tomorrow?" "Where to?" He asked. "The U.K., Swami", I said. "Yes, go", He replied, and walked slowly away. Darshan ended and as I went to sit at the side for a few minutes a man came up to me and quietly said, "This vibhuti is from Swami, take some." As I put my finger into the ash he took some, and again swiped my forehead with it. As he did this, I heard in my head "Goodbye".

It was a sad moment as I walked out of the ashram, but I knew I would be back, and the sad thoughts turned into joy and the excitement of what was to come.

When we got to the airport there were some delays, and we were going to change planes at Bahrain. When we arrived in Bahrain we had missed the connection to London, so we were going to have to wait 15 hours in the airport lounge. After a few minutes a man came in and said "Group of seventeen for London". We went to see what he wanted. He had an air conditioned coach which took us all to a top class hotel where we were given en-suite apartments, one between two, and free food and telephone calls to England. It was a great way to freshen up and see Bahrain. It seemed that Swami had organised a little treat for us on the way home. Thank you Swami.

My parents met me at Heathrow, England still existed and school term was not far away, so back to the unreal world. I sat down in my favourite chair (which was a relief, having sat on the ground for nearly three weeks), and asked "Where to now Swami? Please show me!"

He says that if you take one step towards Him, He will take ten towards you. Swami, I'm running towards you!

HOME AGAIN.......

Having got home there were three weeks left before the end of holidays, so I went down to the south west of France, near to the Pyrenees. This is a fascinating area with lots of spiritual history. I was able to go into Andorra to be with Renu while she recorded part of her new cassette. The beautiful scenery and peace allowed me to gently unwind and muse over my trip to India.

I remember looking out over a beautiful view, in the foreground were the ruins of an old castle, and in the distance as far as the eye could see was a panoramic view of rolling countryside. My little voice said "Look, if you had lived here some six hundred years ago you would have been very proud of that new castle, as it was then, but now it is in ruins. Man-made things pass, yet the sun continues to rise and fall each day over this scene. This routine is unchanged and remains unchanged and gives a good example of why you must try to merge with God at all times and not with man and his creations."

On the way home driving back through France I developed a severe toothache. It got worse and worse until I decided to put into reality some of the things I had learnt in India. I said, "Swami, please help me, this toothache is awful". My little voice told me to pull off the motorway and go into the next small town; as I did I noticed a pharmacy, so I stopped and went in. The lady in the pharmacy could see from my puffed up face that I was in trouble and said she could not give me the antibiotics I needed without a prescription from a dentist; however, I was not to worry because her husband was a dentist across the road and I was to see him immediately. I crossed the road and, sure enough, he saw me straight away, removing the cause of the problem and giving me the vital prescription. Was it coincidence? or was it Swami? There was no doubt in my mind !

Lots of my friends around the country were interested to hear about my trip, and one incident in the west of England was typical of Swami. My friends there wanted to believe in Swami, but somehow, being pillars of the local church, found it difficult to understand how a man in India could have anything to do with their life. They asked me to give a talk three weeks later when I would be in the area. They were at home the next day when an elderly lady who lived in the house behind them called with an aerial photo she had had taken of her house and gardens. She had brought the photo for them to see.......Swami is quite clearly standing on her terrace!!!!!! I have seen the photograph, it is unquestionably Him.

I had taken 10 disposable cameras on my trip to India, and on my return had taken them to a High

Street store to get them developed. They developed 9 and lost the 10th, the film of the Super Speciality Hospital, which needless to say disappointed me greatly. After some negotiation, I contacted their customer relations department and explained the problem. To my relief they were very understanding, and offered to pay my air fare back to India! Naturally, I accepted and wondered what Swami was up to now...........

The weeks went past and the energy that I had felt in India continued to buzz round and round me; then a very special thing happened. My grandmother had slipped into unconciousness and I went to see her on the 20th of November. She was asleep, I asked Swami to look after her and to take her to Him when it was the right moment. He took her on November 23rd which was His birthday. I know that some folk may say that that was total coincidence, but when you come to know more about Swami you realise that this was a loving gesture. It does not matter what is happening around the world, He will still care for each individual in the most intimate way.

The days went past and I found it easier and easier to let go and not to worry about the outcome of events because Swami would be there. Each day I would sit down and talk to Him as if He were in the same room with me and it was amazing the replies or changes in circumstances that happened.

I HAD MY 40th BIRTHDAY ON FEBRUARY 1ST 1995.

I booked my air ticket for March 22nd 1995. This was the last day of school so the 10.15p.m. flight would be possible. My little voice said "book two seats" so I did, not being at all sure of who would be accompanying me. I hoped it would be Rakesh, the accountant who had come with me on the first trip, and who I knew was keen to go again. However, about a month before we were due to go he had an horrific accident in his car! He yelled for Swami and got out completely unscathed, yet his car was in pieces. He then got on the next possible flight to say "thank you" to Swami. Out of the blue another friend, Phil, who had also come on the previous trip telephoned and said that circumstances had suddenly changed and he would like to go to India again. Was I going? The second ticket was taken!

Visa done, injections completed, bags packed, we went to the airport eagerly looking forward to seeing Swami again.

THE INCREDIBLE JOURNEY

This trip, as I was to discover afterwards, had been pre-planned by Swami to the minute. We flew British Airways to Bombay overnight and changed to the domestic airport for the flight to Bangalore where we were met by my dear friend Krishnamurthy. It was great to see him again. He had reserved an hotel for us near the racecourse which was quiet and clean. We shared some Swami experiences and then "crashed out". The next day he joined us for breakfast and organised a taxi to take us on the long drive to Puttaparthi. We bumped along, taking some three and a half hours, getting hotter and hotter as we approached the ashram. We checked in and found the simple flat that another friend in England had arranged for us to use.

It was time for afternoon Darshan, so off we went with me clutching my letter for Swami in my hand, and sat down some seven people away from his walkway. I thought it would be quite impossible to get the letter to Him. However, sitting there, Swami appeared —— what joy, such contentment and happiness. As He approached, a chap sitting next to me pushed me and said "Go on". I lost my balance slightly and, as a result, I had to sit up. Then he pushed me again. Well, I had no choice, I either fell in amongst about eight people or I had to stand up. As I half-stood up to get my balance, Swami looked at me and made His hand gesture to me to give Him the letter, which I did. As I turned away, He said "Where do you come from?" "U.K. Swami". "How many are there of you?" He asked. "Just two" I replied. "Go. go, go," He said.

I looked at Philip and, in a very nervous, excited state, I said "Come on, we've got an interview!" So off we went to wait outside His door. He called another fifteen people from different countries.

We entered the room, which was small with a chair in the corner. I sat down, almost by Swami's right leg. Another man sat to my left between me and His chair. Swami smiled and waved His right hand in the air and a gold ring with nine stones just appeared from nowhere. "For you", He said to the man on my left. "It won't fit", He added, trying to push the ring on to the fourth finger of his left hand. "Try", He said to the man, and then to several others sitting in the room. No way would it go past his knuckle, so Swami held the ring with two fingers, slipped it off and blew on it once, then slipped the ring back on.....a perfect fit. Then He smiled and waved His hand in the air again. It seemed, in slow motion, that a gold bracelet with a watch in it dropped from the centre of His palm...."For you", He said to one of the ladies. "Check the time" He added.....it was correct!

45

Then He asked the first man, "What do you want from me?" "Your blessing, please, Swami," he replied. Swami held His right hand out, palm outwards and said "Here, take my blessing". He smiled, looked at me and said "What is this? What is this?" again with His palm outwards and pointing to me. "I don't know, Swami", I said, somewhat confused. "Pakoda, Pakoda," He said, smiling. "Pakoda?" I queried. "Yes," He said, smiling broadly, "Lots of fat, lots of fat." Everyone laughed. My corpulant tum had caused merriment all round. He then produced a "stone egg"(called a lingam) with another wave of the hand for another lady. "This is for you," He said, "Yes, yes, I know you have cancer. Put this in water and drink two teaspoons of water each day. Cancer gone!" The lady burst into tears. In fact, we all had a tear, sharing the relief and joy of this lady. Then He spoke to some of the others and invited us to go into the inner room in our various groups for more private interviews. Philip and I went in with three Americans, a man and two ladies, one older than the other; I thought perhaps mother and daughter, but they were, in fact, as it turned out later, friends. Swami asked the man what he did. "I run courses for marriage guidance and also spirituality". Swami replied "Marriage with girl merger with God, do not confuse the two". Then He said to the older lady "Where is husband?" "I have no husband." "Where is husband?" He repeated. "I have no husband." Third time...."Where is husband?" "Sorry Swami, I have left husband, I have separated from him in the U.S.A." "Husband good man, go back to him" He said.

Turning to the young lady He said, "you bully husband!" you good woman, husband good man, don't bully, be happy. By which time I knew He was about to come to me and I was getting a bit concerned as to what He might say! However, He looked at me and said "Mind confusion, too much worry of children, school, business, money, mind confusion not good. Health good, mind confusion!" As He spoke, I realised He was speaking with such love and the energy or the feel of the room was fantastic. "What have you brought me?" He asked. Just before the trip I had written a song for Him called "There's only one love". I said "Swami, I have brought you this." He took it, and opened the copy, looked me straight in the eyes and very quietly sang it to me! Tears welled up in my eyes. What greater joy could be given a musician than to have Swami actually sing something he had written. There are not words to express the feeling with which He enveloped me. He turned into the most loving being I had ever seen and if only one could have hugged him! My heart melted.......a bit like that feeling you get if you are a softie over dogs and see some labrador puppies. Then He just looked at me, for what seemed an eternity, but in reality was only a few seconds. The depth of his eyes, they are beautiful. Then He said, "When do you go back?" "April 4th", I replied. "Good, we have time". He

47

got up and we all went back into the other room. Swami then went into His side room and came back holding one of His robes neatly ironed. He gave it to the man on my right, who instantly burst into tears. As I said to Philip after the interview, the experience was the same as Swami giving each one of us a robe, the joy, the disbelief of what we were experiencing. It was just as well He didn't give one to me, however, because it would have been miles too small!!

Out we went on "cloud nine". Philip and I went back to the flat and we both floated round the universe, pinching ourselves, trying to believe what had happened. Night came.....neither of us could sleep, we were surrounded by the most inexpressible feeling. Swami says "bliss" and, really, that is the only word I can find to describe it. We talked throughout the night.

The next morning we went down at 5.30 a.m. to join the Darshan lines, having permission to sit at the front, luckily for me, as it enabled me to stretch my legs for a while before Swami came. He appeared from the womens' side and walked slowly towards us. From about twenty yards away He spotted me. He smiled, and striding up to me said in a loud voice, "Good morning Pakoda, how are you this morning?" Everyone around burst out laughing. How clever He was making this remark; that was His way of introducing us to the people near us who were some of the

48

doctors who worked at the hospitals, professors from the colleges, etc. After He had passed by they all came to me smiling, wanting to know if I knew that Swami's nickname for me meant a south Indian dish with lots of fat! The first person to introduce himself provided water for Swami's farm by means of a windmill. He took us to see Sai Gita, Swami's pet elephant, and then to see the stadium where the huge celebrations are held, Swami's farm, and then to his windmill. The next day Swami passed us smiling, and after Darshan another man introduced himself as Mr. Rao. He had been there since 1958.

He told me that Swami had been standing at the gate of the ashram, and, as he passed, Swami told him to leave the world and come and live in the ashram.....37 years later he was still there! He had watched Swami's reaction to me and said that I should think very seriously because he was certain that Swami had some plan for me. What? Who knows?

The next day Swami came along and, instead of taking a handful of sweets as He normally does from the people sitting offering them for a blessing, He just took four! He then threw one each to a couple of doctors and then one each to Philip and me! After Darshan we went for a walk and I found a tailor to make me some clothes that I wanted for England, and became friendly with two lads who worked there. They, over the next few days, were to take us to

Swami's birthplace, where His parents are buried, and some 15 kilometres away to the school that He went to as a child. All making us feel at home. Just treating us as very close friends, as everyone is to Him.

As the days went past Philip and I took it in turns to sit on the front row and Swami, on several occasions, came near to allow one of us to touch His feet, so beautifully soft and tiny.

Thinking about our visit sitting waiting the following day, I wondered what more I could ask than I already had. Well, there was one thing. As a pianist my dream would be if He would bless my hands so that they could play for Him for ever. I could not ask Him.....He had already given so much. Then I thought, hang on, I will mentally ask Him as He approaches, then that will reassure me once again that there is a mental link as well as the physical.

He approached, walking down the centre of the pathway, looking the other way, back towards me. I thought, looking at His back, "Please Swami, bless my hands...please!" I was already holding my hands as though in prayer (as were most other people). No reaction....He carried on walking slowly, looking away as He passed me. I repeated my thought, then suddenly, still with His back to me and looking away, His right hand shot out from behind Him and took hold of my hands. It seemed an eternity as His hand very, very slowly slid up mine, His fingers touching my fingers until they delicately and so slowly slid off the end of mine. He didn't look at all, yet did such a lovely thing....I'm sorry, I dissolved into floods of tears. There was my Lord here on earth and He had blessed my hands...my dream had come true.

Time flew past, in fact it didn't exist.....those hours waiting for Darshan, sitting on my 30 rupee cushion (somewhat flattened after 10 days use!) were fantastic. Thousands of people just sitting in silence for an hour or more, no-one wanting to talk, only the sound of birds and nature....

On the last day Philip was taken ill with the dreaded tummy bug, and he could not come down with me to Darshan in the morning. I went down and sat in the front line again, and my friend reminded me, if Swami came close, to ask His permission to fly home the following day. Sure enough He came my way. I knelt up and said "Swami, please may I go home tomorrow?" "Where to?" "England Swami." "Yes yes go" He replied. "Great" I thought, He has given His blessing. The people around me pushed me and said "Go on, it's an interview". I thought He had mean't go to England, not for an interview. Reluctantly, I stood up and went round to wait outside His door. There were three other "well built" men there. I sat and waited nervously, expecting to be sent back.

51

Swami came round the corner. "Ah Pakoda", He said, again causing such merriment. "My four pillars" He said, pointing to each of us. We went in with a family of four from Switzerland. He materialised two watches for one of the Swiss boys and his mother. They had leather straps and His head on the face which changed colour as the watch was moved through different angles. This time He did not speak to us as a group at all. He just took each group into the inner room separately. I waited patiently, thinking of all the questions I might ask Him if I had the opportunity. Previously emotion got in the way. This time however, sheer joy overwhelmed me. Eventually, having seen everyone else, He beckoned me. I stood up. He smiled, "Too much cheese, too much sweet," He added referring to my tum. I went in followed by Swami. He turned to face me and I wondered what was going to happen. What did occur was the greatest moment of my life.

He took my left hand with His left hand, looking straight into my eyes. My eyes were transfixed by His, so lovingly deep, yet transmitting so much energy. Then He started thumping my chest quite firmly with the palm of his right hand and He said, "Swami loves you......Swami always with you......Swami never leave you."

He must have thumped me 15 times and my chest seemed swirling with energy. My mind went completely blank, and the most all pervading feeling came over me.....yes, His Love. I seemed to be floating on air, as big as the world, yet it was beyond joy. There are again no words to express it fully. I just hope that everyone has the opportunity to share this experience.

How could I ask about healing work, family, future, past lives, Christ, when He had just promised never to leave me. I had all the time in the world to ask Him when I got home, in the stillness and quiet, and then to prepare my thoughts properly. He repeated "Mind confusion, money, school, business......you not married....not good..... Swami find you wife, good wife......yes, Swami find you good wife." "Thank you Swami" I muttered humbly. I was nearly speechless. He took me by the elbow as if to say that was all. A thought suddenly rushed through me and I said "Swami, please can I ask you something?""Yes ask". "Swami, please will you forgive me all the things I have done wrong in this life that I have known about, all the things that I have done wrong that I have not known about, and also in all my previous lives." He looked at me and gently slapped me on my shoulder. "Forgiven", He said. A sense of tremendous relief came over me. Suddenly, all the past seemed to fade away and I was given a clean slate again......but what a responsibility.

I met my new friend Mr Rao again and he said that, despite what I might think, I must walk around the statue of Ganesha (the Elephant God) at least three times before I left the ashram. Ganesha was apparently a remover of obstacles in one's life. I also had to take back to England a photo of Ganesha. The following morning I did walk round the statue three times, but the shop was closed, so I could not get a photograph of Ganesha. Our taxi took us straight to Krishnamurthy's house in Bangalore, where we had lunch with him and his family.

I had received an invitation from some friends of Krishnamurthy to speak about my experiences with, and how I had found, Swami. This meeting was at another Mandir (Temple) in Bangalore, not far from the airport.

Everyone was very appreciative, and after the talk I was presented with a small present which I thought might be a cassette of Swami's discourses. However, time was desperately short to get to the airport, so I did not open it until I got on to the plane. It was a lovely carved statue of Ganesha in sandelwood! Surprise! Surprise! He had thought of everything.

The homeward journey was good and it was great to arrive back in England, but, somehow I was still connected with Puttaparthi.

Swami had proved His grace and love again because, just before we had left for India, my father had had a medical problem diagnosed, and was awaiting news of a possible operation. Unbeknown to anyone but myself I had given Swami a letter on the day I had arrived at Puttaparthi. In the letter I had asked Him to heal my father. Now had come the time to go back to the specialist to have the final verdict, which was "All clear"....blood count normal.....no problems!!! No treatment needed........ THANK YOU SWAMI!.

THE WORLD MUSIC FESTIVAL

Having returned home, what next? The telephone rang, it was Aime Levy, the Co-ordinator for the Sai Organization in England. He wanted to ask me to play the piano at Puttaparthi in July for an International Music Festival. The idea was that England would present an example of a classical recital on the piano, and then a typical folksong from England, Ireland, Scotland, and Wales. Would I play Clare de Lune by Debussy, The Prelude in G minor by Rachmaninoff, and then accompany Melanie, a lovely flute player from London, in a piece by Mozart.

What a brilliant request. I suddenly remembered the letter I had written nine months previously at Whitefield asking whether I could play for Swami, and now out of the blue I was being asked to play. Everything was agreed, and I was to fly out to India straight after the end of term concert at school so that I would arrive one day before the two day event. The only problem was the piano. Where would I find a good piano in India? I contacted various Embassies, the Arts Attache, the larger hotels, all the shops in Bangalore to no avail. Then a piano tuner said that he could supply a one year old Yamaha upright piano, as new. This seemed a safe solution, so we agreed to the terms of hire and removal.

Having got all the arrangements finalised, my parents decided that they wanted to come and see what I had found, to make sure I had not got involved with some funny weird cult and also to see the Music Festival. So, having had all the necessary jabs, cases stuffed full of loo rolls, immodium, paracetamol, and mosquito- bite spray, we set off for India. Heathrow-Bombay, then the internal flight over to Bangalore where we were met by my friend Krishnamurthy again. We stayed the first night in a hotel in Bangalore.

My mother was rather horrified by the poverty and disgusting conditions in which people lived, especially in the shanty towns. Our taxi took us to Puttaparthi, and, on arrival at the ashram, we went to our allotted flat, and settled in. I then anxiously went to find my piano! To my horror, they had delivered a piano that was over 100 years old with half the notes not working! What was I to do? The technicians had found a Clavinova, which is an electric piano, but luckily they could not get it to work, as it would have been very difficult to play the Rachmaninoff on this keyboard.

The organisers hunted round, and they found a baby grand piano in the Primary School just down the road. This was delivered onto the stage, I looked at it, and realised there was something missing. There were no pedals, not even the wooden supports!

I telephoned the piano tuner in Bangalore to ask him and his son to come immediately to sort out the problem. They worked all night, with the help of Aime, and were able eventually to make up a bracket affair, so that I had one pedal, the right hand sustain pedal, which worked. The piano was hopelessly out of tune, so they tuned it, it must have been at least six times. Some of the other countries decided to use an electric keyboard, but this was hopeless for me, so I decided that come what may I would play the piano.

The afternoon came, and the concert started in the Poornachandra Hall, which seats some 20,000 people. This was packed to capacity, and there were television relays to those people outside and those seated in the Mandir itself. Swami came and sat in the centre front, and the concert started with the American contribution, followed by us.

I sat at the piano, and Stewart, who was going to play the guitar and sing folksongs with Sarah, announced my programme; the curtain went up and I struck the first notes of the Rachmaninoff Prelude. As I did so, the piano dropped more and more out of tune.... what was I to do? My mind raced, as the Rachmaninoff was a loud fast piece and it was going to sound awful. I nearly changed the piece into "The Entertainer", as that would have sounded great on what was now a real Honky Tonk! I played on..... Luckily, the local Indian section of the audience was

58

not used to a piano and were fascinated by my use of my left hand, as in India keyboards or small harmoniums are played with the right hand and pumped with the left; so to see me play with both hands was a new experience.

I could have cried.....I desperately wanted to play my best for Swami, and this was happening. I mentally called to Swami "HELP!" When I started to play the Clare de Lune, suddenly the piano was back in reasonable tune, and the Mozart which followed was superb. I thought this was my imagination until I heard the result on the video which confirms what happened! Having played my pieces I then introduced Sarah and Stewart, who ended their selection with "Irish eyes are smiling" to which Swami and the whole audience clapped along.

The rest of the concert was very interesting, each country presenting a selection of music and dance from their culture. At the end of the first day, everyone who had performed came on stage for the traditional Aarthi. I was at the back, still wearing my black tails in which I had performed. Swami lit the flame and then walked round the artists directly towards me. I realised that I was standing near the door that led to His private rooms. He came up to me and tweaked my cheek saying " Very happy".

The next afternoon I decided to stay back stage, as it was cooler and I could sit on a chair rather than on the floor. Another very interesting afternoon, and at the end of it I thought that I would wait again by His door. Everyone else was singing the finale song and into the Aarthi again. Swami came round beaming, He was so happy, everyone else was facing forward and did not see what the two "naughty boys" were up to! He held His hands face downwards, mine were facing upwards and He kept on tapping mine saying "Very Happy! Very Very Happy!" smiling that wonderful smile, then away He went.

All the performers were called the following morning at 7.30. to go into the Poornachandra Hall, in costume, as Swami wanted to have a photograph taken with each country. We arrived and sat down in our country groups and Swami came in and spoke to each country separately. What joy it was to see Him so happy. Swami came to us and just put His hand on my shoulder and said "I will give you a special interview". My heart leapt with eager anticipation. Then we went up on to the stage for a photograph and yes! I was going to stand beside Him. He smiled and held my hand, and the energy that seemed to flow through was tremendous. Another wonderful moment of my life. Everyone was happy that the Festival had been a success, and Swami was happy and so loving.

MANDIR AT NIGHT

THE BLESSINGS

SRI SATHYA SAI SUPER SPECIALITY HOSPITAL

THE MUSEUM

ADMINISTRATIVE BUILDING, UNIVERSITY

DHARSAN IN WHITEFIELD

**STEWART, AIME (front), ME, SWAMI, SARAH, MELANIE
AT THE MUSIC FESTIVAL**

A SPEECH IN THE MANDIR

WHERE IS WIFE?

WITH MAYNARD FERGUSSON

BAND BOYS, CHRISTMAS '95

A SECTION OF STUDENT CHOIR AND DEVOTEES

CHRISTMAS DAY WITH SWAMI

THE BAND BOYS WITH SWAMI

SANDALWOOD GANESH

The next thing I knew was that Aime and the American Co-ordinator wanted to speak to me quietly. Swami had asked me to speak that afternoon in the Mandir before His own discourse. He had asked that I should express my feelings about the Music Festival, what I had learnt and experienced. What JOY! What shall I say? Then I remembered what Swami had said to Isaac Tigrett when He had sent Him to speak at The United Nations ——"Go to your room, be quiet, listen, and I will do everything". So I went back to my flat and, as I entered, the little voice in my head (Swami!) said "Start off by telling them about sitting in the lines at Whitefield last year and writing to Swami asking if it be possible, may I play for you. One year later, here I am . Now grab a pencil, and write down the following on which to end."

Swami.
Please take our hands that we may play for You,
Take our voices that we may sing for You,
Take our bodies that we may dance for You,
So that when we return to our own countries we
    may be channels of Your love throughout all
    the world!

Then, I sat quietly totally relaxed for a couple of hours. Swami had asked that I should wear my black tails again, so I went down to the Mandir half an hour early. I was given a chair near the veranda. The

61

Mandir was full and I was told afterwards that that crowd was nearly 200,000 people, they seemed to be everywhere. Swami walked in and came up to me, and said" Are you going to speak this afternoon?" "Yes Swami" "For how long?" He asked. "About 8 minutes Swami" I replied. "Good" He said, and went to His chair and sat down. The proceedings started, and I was introduced by the American Co-ordinator. I had been told that I must go up to Swami, kneel down and touch His feet, then to say the formal introduction.

I went up to Swami, knelt down, and, although I loved Him and wanted to share that love, I felt in me that I could not touch His feet. This however was a formal occasion, therefore I must show respect and do the correct thing. Having knelt down, He took my hands, which were aiming for His feet , and He said " No need, no need", and He gave me one of his understanding smiles. I got up, went to the rostrum and spoke. I didn't know what I had said until I saw the video later on. The only thing that I remembered at the time was calling Swami " My greatest friend". This was then to give me one of the lessons of the trip.

When I had finished speaking, I went back to Swami, who patted me on the back and smiled that lovely smile. I returned to my place and shortly afterwards Swami beganHis discourse. Unfortunately, I was sitting between two speakers, and with the slight distortion I could not understand what He was saying even with Anil Kumar translating into English. Suddenly, everyone was looking at me, but I did not understand why. Afterwards I listened to the cassette recording of the discourse and Swami had suddenly made reference to my calling Him My Greatest Friend, and then went on to say that God is your Greatest Friend. He said there are two types of friends, the new friends who you invite to your home but to whom you still offer all your proper respect and are polite and yet reserved to. Your Greatest Friend is the friend with whom you share all your life, your problems, your great times, in fact everything, you do not hold anything back at all. So, treat GOD as YOUR OLDEST AND GREATEST FRIEND.....ALWAYS.

SURPRISE AFTER SURPRISE

The next morning I went down to go in to the lines as usual, and they stopped me at the entrance and said "Sai Ram Sir, verandah, verandah!" I didn't really understand so I waited, and the Italian Conductor who had spoken after me the previous afternoon arrived and they said, the same thing to him. We looked at each other somewhat confused. They then told us to come back in half an hour and join the doctors and teachers on the verandah outside the door of Swami's interview rooms. What a treat! We were still nervous, and eventually we followed in, both of us still thinking there had been some mistake. However, we were welcomed on to the verandah and I was given a position on the back wall only about seven places from His door. Swami walked around and when He arrived on the verandah He invited Isaac Tigrett, and two or three American colleagues with him, into the interview room. The door shut. About four minutes later the door opened and Swami beckoned me to come. Another interview — is it possible? Swami said "Come and sit here" right beside him. He was holding a small gold ring vertically between two of His fingers, and it had a small diamond on the top. Swami asked "What is this?" "It's looks like a diamond ring Swami", I said meekly. "Looks like, looks like???" He said, and then threw it to one of the Americans. "What is it?" He asked again. The American replied "A diamond ring, Swami." "Good"

64

Swami said, " This man (pointing to the other American) does not like it". Then, holding the ring about a foot from my eyes, He blew on it three times, and the diamond turned on the third blow into an oblong green Emerald, and the casing changed on the ring. His fingers were nowhere near the stone at any point!?!? "Now do you like it?" Swami asked, "Yes" he said.

"Now" said Swami, looking at me, "What would you like? Anything, anything you wish!" I was stunned, it was the last thing I was expecting Swami to say. I just completely seized up! Swami waved His right hand in the air in a clockwise circular motion and under His hand in mid-air appeared the most astonishingly huge diamond ring. "Give me the fourth finger of your left hand. It will fit. He slid it on and it was fantastic, a perfect fit. I could not believe my eyes. Swami, having given Isaac Tigrett an interview, took me into the inner room, where He repeated that I was still somewhat confused in my head and that I must let everything go. I needed a wife, so He would find one for me! After a few more personal comments He asked when I would be going home, so I said my ticket was booked for the 24th, but please could I stay until the 14th of the following month? "Yes" He said, "This is your home, come and go as you please, THIS is your home."

I left the interview room on cloud nine!

I was so pleased that my parents had come on the trip as they had seen me go into the interview room "empty handed" and come out with the ring, otherwise I am certain they would not have believed me!

My parents had come for two weeks, so I asked if my father could be with me on the verandah to which the powers that be kindly agreed. They were due to fly back to England on July 20th. July 19th was my mother's birthday, and their wedding anniversary, so my father took a small container with some cloves (we had been told that Swami liked to be offered a clove on peoples' birthdays), and a rose for Him to bless. Swami came up to him, took a clove, ate it, and then blessed the rose and enquired "When do you leave?" "Tomorrow morning" we both replied. "Good, I will see, I will see" He said, and walked away. An interview for my parents? Great!

The next morning came, the taxi had been booked to go to Bangalore at 7.30 a.m. We went down to their last Darshan. Swami walked round, took some people for interview, but not us. Puzzled, we waited. My father was concerned about missing the flight and I knew my mother would be worrying, so in the end and against my better judgement - having read so many similar stories - my father and I agreed to leave. I went with them to Bangalore and saw them off, then returned to Puttaparthi by mid evening.

As soon as I arrived back, everyone I saw came running up to me asking" Where were you this morning? Swami was looking for you four times! He sent students to your room, where were you???????" I could have cried. Why didn't we wait, why didn't we wait — why? why? why? What a lesson in trust!

The next day Swami didn't look at me. In the afternoon He was out in His car and I was walking down towards the college. I was alone on this stretch of road, so I bent down to wave to Him; He saw me, and raising both hands He waved back smiling. Was I forgiven, I wondered? The following morning He came up on the verandah, looked at me and beckoned to me to come. I got up, and in a loud voice, amusing the students, He said, "And where were you the day before yesterday —— chasing women in Bangalore?" "No Swami" I spluttered, "I was taking my parents........." "I find you wife, Swami finds you wife". "But Swami, I was taking my parents to the airport". "Yes I know, I joke......too fat.....one heart, two bodies!" He quipped.

SWAMI ON THE VERANDAH
AND HIS STUDENTS

I changed my return booking, so that I could stay six weeks until August 14th. I was very content. I met my very good friend Mr Rao each day to discuss the things that had happened.

Swami asked me to teach his physics master how to play the piano. They had now got the electric piano repaired. There was also a college Band that plays on special occasions, and He asked me to help the Bandboys. What fun we had, the boys were brilliant, so kind, intelligent and receptive, in fact they were like blotting paper lapping up everything that I had to teach them. They learned how to read music the western way and how to do their own arrangements for the Band.

The greatest problem was getting any printed music. In Bangalore I found the one and only music book, which in fact was superb as it had a large selection of popular classics arranged for piano, which we could easily rearrange for the Band. They loved "Land of hope and glory", "The New World Symphony"- or the theme from it! - by Dvorak, and "Roses from the South" by Strauss. One day I asked them how close they wanted to come to Swami as He was five foot three and I had arranged that popular jazz tune" Five foot two, eyes of blue" for them.....only an inch in it! They loved the idea of syncopation and jazz. Then Swami asked me to give a talk to all the students, some 700 of them, about the piano and my music. One evening I went down to the hostel where all the boys stay. They had set up the electric piano with a video camera focused on my left hand, and had linked the camera to television screens down the room so that the boys could see my left hand play. I wondered how I could relate the many different styles possible on the piano to the students, from Classics, Jazz, Romantic to "Slush" and Ragtime. I had a brainwave; relate it to the silent Black and White Films. They loved films, and they thought that this was brilliant with lots of fun imitating the chases," love at first sight" scenes, rescues, romantic drives etc., allowing me to demonstrate all styles. We had a great evening, and, again, they were so kind and appreciative.

Sitting on the verandah a couple of mornings later, Swami came round and He had a very serious look on His face. You could have heard a pin drop, everyone wondered who it was going to be.............yes, He beckoned me. I got up, He looked very very serious as I walked towards Him. I could sense the other doctors and teachers thinking "I'm glad it's you and not me!" Swami slowly looked me up and down, then His eyes rested on my "tum" and He said, grinning like mad, "And how many months, and how many months?" I guffawed with laughter, and so did

69

everyone else. Swami laughed out loud, too, which was lovely. I sat down again chuckling. One of the elderly gentlemen there came up to me afterwards and said that my English name was David but in India it ought to be Goliath!

It was a tremendous experience to see the love pour out from Swami, His care and attention to every detail. He always talked to the doctors who worked at the hospitals and gave advice about individual cases, producing vibhuti, and even tablets for individual patients. Then He would turn to some of the students and talk with them, always giving advice, then passing through us all making kind loving remarks, as He did to me, putting His hand on my shoulder saying"Are you happy here?" "Yes Swami" I replied. "Good, all I want is for you to be happy," and moved on.

There is always the loving !ook from those eyes that, when you look into them, is almost as though you are looking into eternity or into the heavens. He is only five foot three and very slight, yet His form changes from the loving teacher and leader to the grandad with the "naughty boy" sense of humour and a tremendous twinkle in the eyes.

Inevitably, reactions to the photographs of him vary, and some people find Him difficult to relate to with His orange robe and black fuzzy hair, yet, when you see Him "in the flesh", He is instantly lovable.

The days rolled by, the joy of watching Swami every day, the thrill of time and time again seeing His love being given to someone else, their smile, their tear and His Grace. One of the greatest experiences I found was feeling and sharing someone else's joy when they had spoken to, or had had an interview with, Swami. To share in the real living experience of His love, in whatever form, is certainly the most marvellous thing in my life.

HOME OR AWAY?

I flew home on August 14th, and on the way caught the most glorious cold which turned into 'flu and got so bad that my doctors tested for malaria. It took several weeks to recover fully and I discovered that my parents had been quite ill on their return too. I wondered why I had come back to England, until the Barclaycard bill came in! Yes, back to work. My own concerts re-started very well, and then my redundancy from the school job was confirmed........O.K. Swami.......where to now? Had I come home to England, or had I come away? Inside I desperately wanted to go Home again! It became clear that I could go back out again at half term for a week or a fortnight. I asked Swami mentally whether I should go for one or two weeks, and please would He guide me as to which.

I was with my parents at the time and my mother came in and asked me to telephone a number left on the answer-phone. It was a coach operator wanting to book a lot of tickets for a show which, if I did the show, would limit me to one week in India, and actually provide the finance for me to go.

Inside me, I must be honest, I was concerned that having had such a fantastic trip in the summer, would this trip be a disappointment? Would I be allowed on the verandah again? The college boys had been so appreciative, and had said "Please, please come back soon", but in England when we say thank you very much, please come again, we do not always mean it!

So, yes, I knew that I could not lose my feelings for Swami, the ashram, and the friends that I had made there, but was it really necessary to go back again, was I pushing my luck? I was hoping to start planning the following years work, and that could depend on whether I would return to the ashram once, twice, or more the next year.

If Swami wanted me to go, of course I'd be there like a shot, but supposing it was my ego getting in the way? The only way to find out would be to make a quick visit and at least help the Bandboys. I booked up to fly out on October 26th returning on November 2nd 1995.

WELCOME HOME!

Two days before I left England I received a fax from the Bandboys asking when would I be coming again. Great, I thought, the first sign that they really did want me back. The trip was perfect and again my good friend Krishnamurthy met me in Bangalore. Together with his wife and her sister from New Zealand, we went to Puttaparthi the next day, having rested overnight in Bangalore.

On the way to Puttaparthi I was taken off the main road to another one of Swami's schools, and to a lovely Mandir, just on the edge of some mountains. The headmaster showed us round, ending up in the school hall, on the long side of which was a very large photograph of Swami. They smiled at me as I looked at it, because Swami is sitting in a chair looking towards you with His feet crossed.......the right foot facing you on top of His left foot. As I walked down the hall, I had the sense of someone following me...........it was Swami in the photograph.........He follows you up and down the hall.........and so does his right foot, which at the other end of the hall is facing the other end!!!!! I walked up and down 20 times trying to fathom it out.....one time I even ran trying to beat Him...but no! It is only a photograph that you can touch, yet He moves on it.........?!

We arrived at Puttaparthi, what a lovely feeling of peace, and I'm home again. We went to the flat, unpacked, and I went down to go in for Darshan. A college boy spotted me, and within a couple of minutes all the Bandboys were there giving me a tremendous welcome. I approached the line to go onto the verandah, and saw some familiar faces, who again instantly recognised me. "Where shall I go this time?" I asked. Without a flicker of doubt they all said my place was on the verandah, and don't ask because it is for life! My inside turned over, with relief. Yes I am at home, and I am really looking forward to seeing Swami.

All the students and teachers were there from Bangalore College helping with the preparations for the Birthday celebrations, so the verandah was quite full and I was sitting further away from Swami's door than before. This did not matter, I was amongst friends.

Swami appeared the other side of the Mandir and walked through, first past the women and then the men and then across the students. It was lovely to see Him again. He walked up to the verandah and round His pillar by His door. He looked straight at me, and asked "And when did you come?" My heart leapt with joy.......yes, He had remembered me.....how stupid of me, my "monkey mind", but being honest, I had wondered, with all the Universe to look after, whether He would show any reaction to me. "This morning" I replied. "Where is your black jacket? (He was referring to my black tails in the summer) Come!" I stood up and walked towards Him. I had taken a few letters from friends in England. He took them and tapped me on my "tum" and said "Too fat, Too fat." "Swami, I have tried so many things, what do I do now?" He looked at me and then away into eternity, then He looked me straight in the eyes and said, "Stop eating completely!" We all laughed and He put His hand on my shoulder as if to say that's all for now, sit down, which I did.

The next few days were terrific; a couple of hours in the morning and in the evening I spent with the Bandboys rehearsing Marches, Happy Birthday, and the new Lotus Waltz that I had written for them. They worked so hard, the results proved their determination to play their best for Swami.

On my last morning I went as usual down to Darshan, and I took with me my new cassette called "Pure Gold" which is a selection of popular classical pieces for the piano. I hoped that Swami might bless it .

Having completed the interviews, Swami opened the door, and glided out into the middle of the verandah, stopping just two people away from me. He stood there emanating love and making gentle remarks to the students, and giving advice to the doctors and teachers. It was a joy just sitting there watching, and listening. Suddenly, He looked at me and said "Come Pakoda, what have you brought for me?" I approached Swami, and eagerly told Him that I had brought Him my new cassette. "Oh good, Pure Gold" He said, tapping it against His left arm, and then against me. Smiling He said, "This is plastic, not Gold!!" "I know Swami" I said, "I played these pieces thinking of you, it's western classical music for the piano." "Yes" He said, "We need to find wife don't we? ....everyone laughed......"What would you like?" He teased. "Tall? Medium? or Small?" "Swami, please will you choose for me, you know best, please!" "No, no, you choose, how about Medium?.........England and Italy go well together, how would you like an Italian girl?" "Yes please Swami". Suddenly, He switched back to the cassette He was still holding. "Is this for me?" He asked. "Yes Swami". My mind raced, I was going to have the chance, so go for it! "Please have it as a tiny Birthday present from me, and, as I cannot be here for your Birthday, can I wish you very Happy Birthday." ....GREAT!.... I'd done it! I'd been able to wish Him personally "Happy Birthday"- another dream come true. He smiled and said "Happy, I'm always happy, please be happy.....this cassette, is it for me?""Yes Swami". "Then I would like to keep it, may I?" So gentle and kind, not only had He held it and blessed it, He was going to keep it!

Then He placed His hand on my shoulder and quietly said "I will talk". I sat down in a complete daze. I had never thought that Swami would keep the tape. As I sat there day-dreaming about how fantastic this trip was, Swami walked through the students and passed just in front of me; I was not really concentrating when He suddenly turned and said, "I will talk, what is your programme?" "I go tomorrow morning" I replied. "Good, then I will speak this evening." I couldn't believe my ears, but perhaps He meant in my dreams, or something. That evening, I went down to Darshan and waited quietly in my usual place . Swami came out and walked round. He picked some Australians for an interview, and then chose an Indian family. The first part of the next incident I did not see, as I was sitting behind a pillar, so I have to rely on my friends who did see for the details. The first thing that I experienced was that everyone in the Mandir was clapping and cheering. Swami had called this Indian family along with a very very elderly lady, who was in a wheelchair. The family started to push her towards Swami, when He apparently said "No, walk!" This lady got up from out of the wheel-chair, the first time for 15 years we discovered, and walked elegantly up to the interview room and entered inside. This next part I saw. The door closed, and, as Swami had promised He would talk to me, I knew I must wait. I was not going off to have any "tiffen"! The moment I stopped thinking, the door opened and Swami was standing there......"Come Pakora, come." I went in and the elderly lady was sitting on the floor. I honestly thought that this was, to put it mildly, unwise. I sat next to her. Swami made some vibhuti for us, and then took the Australians in for their private interview. What happened next was a moment that I shall never forget in all my life. Swami invited the Indian family into the inner room. The two sons came to help the elderly lady up off the floor. "No no" Swami said, "Bhagavan here." He raised His hands in the air, palms pointing down towards her, and I find the following few moments very difficult to put into words. As I was sitting beside her I <u>felt</u> exactly what happened. Energy poured out of His hands in a kind of circular motion, it was not like an electrical energy, it was sheer love, so power-ful, it was almost a glimpse of Heaven. I burst into floods of tears, I couldn't help it, the feeling was so beautiful. The elderly lady got up like a three year old and went into the inner room. After some time they reappeared, and Swami took me in for my interview. He talked about many personal things, again promis-ing me a wife. Then He said, "Every evening you sit down in your chair and talk to me, sometimes you are cross with me, sometimes you are angry with me, I know, I know, this is good, give everything to me. <u>Swami is in you, around you and with you, always give Him everything!</u>"

He showed, as always, such love and care. We came out into the outer room, to join the others. I sat down. Swami talked again to the others, then suddenly turned to me and said "What would you like, anything!" I couldn't believe my ears, I looked at Swami, my heart said "Just your love and protection Swami." He waved His right hand in the air, and, slowly, from about 4 inches under His hand in mid-air appeared the most beautiful Japamala (rather like a set of rosary beads, with 108 beads) in silver and crystal. He put it round my neck and said, "Do you know what this is?" "No Swami, I don't know." He looked at me, and very gently said "This is Divine Protection." This statement from Swami seemed to open a great deep feeling of beauty inside me. Suddenly I felt completely safe, and an extraordinary peace welled up within me ("That peace which passes all understanding" ??).

We went outside and I sat down. Swami had tucked the Japamala inside my shirt. Everyone was anxious to know what had happened, they could tell something had happened because, apparently, they could see it on my face. Swami then walked through the Temple and came out the other end, very close to me. He looked at me and smiled and said "Well, where is it then?" I got out the Japamala. "Gosh!" He said, "Where did you buy that?" He walked away swinging an imaginary Japamala like a naughty Boy. Having walked through the students He again returned to me. He stood directly in front of me. I looked into His eyes, and I realized that every part of me had joined with Him a marvellous feeling. He stayed there, I put my hands together, and said what I had wanted to say for a very long time. Not the "thankyou" for the gifts, health, life etc, but a real THANK YOU, slow...... sincere...... from the soul, for Being, for finding me and all of us. I had the chance and I said it very, very slowly. I knew He knew what I meant. He put His hand on my head and stayed there; for another minute or so. It seemed like eternity. Then He whispered, with a lovely question mark in His voice, very very slowly, "Why?" and He glided away.

I knew that this was the end of the chapter for this trip.........what a trip!...........

I left for England again.

I'M DREAMING OF A SAI CHRISTMAS!

Back in my familiar comfortable (large) chair, I sat thinking over the previous few days. Everything I had wanted to be confirmed had been confirmed to me. I was at "home" with Swami, I did have a real opportunity to teach the students about western music, and I was learning more and more about who and what Sai Baba really is. I held the ring, and stopped my monkey mind racing thinking that it was all one big dream. The ring and the Japamala were real, I could hold them, so the whole situation was very real.

Within me I wanted to go back again (surprise, surprise!). I would love to spend Christmas and New Year there. I had no concerts booked, so I could go back straight after the end of the school term. I inwardly hoped that there would be an opportunity to help the college Bandboys with their music. I had seen videos of previous Christmass when the famous jazz trumpet player Maynard Ferguson had been there —— perhaps music at Christmas was his responsibility, so I must realise that I may have to listen this time.

I seemed to be much calmer within myself, and was content to live life day by day without making major plans, despite the knowledge that I was redundant from the end of December. My mind seemed to be in a sort of daze, yet school went on succesfully ending the term with a superb carol service. I had an inner knowing, that I could not explain, that everything would be alright, and I must not make any plans for the future.

I had booked my flight to Bombay on the 16th of December and had budgeted the normal cost within my now very limited finances. On the last Friday of term I contacted my travel agent to arrange collection of my ticket and to my horror, the ticket was £250 more than before due to it being the Christmas period. I went back to my room and sat quietly, and had a "talk" to Swami. Was this His way of saying do not come? If so I would accept the sign, but if not PLEASE HELP as a further £250 was not there. I could only leave the situation in His hands.

The next morning I went into the staff room at school and, as usual, there was a pile of letters for me. I opened them and, to my sheer amazement, there was a letter from a great follower of Sai Baba, living across country, who certainly did not know my detailed finances. The letter said that as I was going to Puttaparthi at Christmas to help the students with their music, so would I please accept the enclosed cheque towards the airfare. This was a cheque for £250.!!!!!!!

83

I confirmed my ticket and the time passed quickly, so I was soon sitting on the overnight flight to Bombay and then, as usual, to Bangalore where it was so good to be "home" again with my dear friend Krishnamurthy, and his wife and family. I soon caught up with the latest Swami news, especially of his close experiences with Swami at his 70th Birthday celebrations. There were apparently hundreds of thousands present for the 14 day celebrations and one of the most incredible things that Krishnamurthy told me was that during the whole of this time free food was provided 3 times a day for everyone. The logistics of this is, to me, mind boggling. He said that the bowls never seemed to empty....... Where does one start preparing such quantities? I just wonder whether we have experienced another example of the Bible story of the two loaves and five fishes that fed the thousands, years ago?

The next day the taxi bounced us along the now familiar roads to Puttaparthi. There was an inner glow as we rounded the corner to drive the last kilometre or so down the colourful bush-lined smooth stretch of road between the college and school down to the Ashram. I registered, and went to find the familiar flat again.

As time for afternoon Darshan approached I went down to join the "Regulars" waiting to go on to the verandah. I was thrilled to meet Maynard Ferguson,

84

who had arrived a few days earlier to - as I had thought - to help with the music at Christmas. It was instantly clear that we were going to have a great time together. The students had delicately tried to describe me to Maynard, unable to remember which of us had the larger "TUM". We both agreed that there was not much in it! As an old hand in show business he had a terrific sense of humour, so we were in for a lot of fun.

We went in and it was lovely to see Swami again. He walked straight down tome, took all the letters I had brought from England, and then introduced me to my "Brother", Maynard of course, gesturing that our tums matched in size! Then He said, "where is wife?" We all smiled.......here we go again....off Swami went smiling.

After Darshan and bhajans we went down to the college to meet the Bandboys. It was great to be back with them, their attitude is so kind and appreciative, let alone their keenness to learn and play well. Maynard had his trumpet with him, wow! what a player! The Bandboys had organized an electric piano for me, so we were able to sort out some new arrangements for Christmas Day between us. We were like a "Double Act" teaching the Bandboys. They loved it, and so did we! All the old jokes about music were coming out, we had such fun. We decided that we would play Frosty the Snowman, Rudoph the red-nosed Reindeer, a Carol medley, Choral and Allegro, finishing with Jingle Bells. The next few days before Christmas we went down to be with the Band every morning and evening to rehearse. In the meantime, the western visitors were organising a choir to sing in the Mandir in the afternoon of Christmas eve, and a sort of Christmas nativity play was being prepared for Christmas Eve in the Poornachandra hall.

Every day Maynard and I sat next to each other constantly smiling, finding such pleasure in life. Swami kept coming past, or looking at us with His knowing smile, and of course making remarks about my "wife". He called the Bandboys and us for an interview to talk about the music for Christmas and then, in front of them, said that He would find a wife for me and marry me. The boys loved this, and very soon the whole college was looking for a wife for me too!

Christmas day arrived and started with everyone coming down to the Mandir early, each with a lighted candle, and walking round the Mandir singing carols. Swami came out onto the balcony wearing a white robe and gave His blessing to everyone. This was by any standard a very beautiful moment with the thousands of lighted candles and the lights of the Mandir itself making a superb setting for Swami. The Band had to be set up in the centre of the Mandir by 7.30 a.m. We connected the electric piano and waited for Swami to come out again. He had told me that I should wear my black tails again, which should have been returned to England by some friends after the Birthday celebrations, but had been forgotten, so they were there still in Puttaparthi! Maynard sat beside me as he was going to play with the Band and conduct some of the pieces.

I had had one of the local tailors make some Santa hats in red with white tassels, one for each of the Bandboys. They were at first worried that Swami would not approve, but we assured them that it was Christmas morning and we had done them in love for Swami; so, once Swami had come in, the Boys stood up ready to play wearing these hats. The whole place rang with laughter and applause of approval as Swami walked down to them smiling and saying "Monkeys, Monkeys". The Mandir then resounded with some splendid music, very well played by the boys, and everyone clapped along while Maynard and I joined in with the Ragtime arrangements.

Swami was smiling and everyone seemed very happy. When we had finished this section Maynard and I were invited to sit beside Swami, but I had to go back to the piano as the students had asked me to play with them in the selection of songs chosen and organised by their physics master. He played the keyboard very well and there was bass and lead guitar and drum kit. This too was great fun.

Swami had given me the greatest Christmas present of my life by allowing me to help with the music. I was very very happy.

HAS ANYBODY SEEN MY GAL?

New year approached and Swami gave permission for us to present another short music programme with the Band on the morning of January 1st. Maynard and I continued to go down to the hostel every morning and evening to teach the Bandboys yet more new arrangements.

One evening I shall never forget. I was walking towards the boys' Hostel where we were going to rehearse, and as often is the case Sai Gita, Swami's pet elephant, was out on the road taking her evening stroll. Suddenly, all the lights went out and everything was plunged into pitch darkness with an electricity cut. There was no moon, and my eyes did not adjust to the blackness. I could see nothing. I knew that the road was straight, but I also remembered that there was an elephant not far ahead wandering in that road. So I proceeded very slowly, with my arms outstretched in front of me, to ward off a possibly most undignified encounter! I felt a complete fool, and was only glad that no-one could see me! I eventually arrived at the Hostel when the lights came on again——Sai Gita had crossed the road in the darkness, so I _had_ missed her, thank goodness.

New Years day arrived, and we took our places as at Christmas in the Mandir. We began the selection of music with an arrangement for the Band from one of

Maynard's albums "Gospel John". This lively jazz arrangement set the scene for a fresh exciting new year. They then played the theme from Dvorak's New World Symphony so gently that there were a few magical moments of silence after the last chord died away before rousing applause. Maynard and I played a duet which was our arrangement of the old Nat King Cole hit........"Unforgettable *that's* what you are". We dedicated this especially to Swami.

Then we all played a Dixieland arrangement of the song Five foot two. I was inwardly amused, sitting there playing this for Swami thinking that we were musically within one inch of Him. Swami in the meantime was sitting there smiling at *me*; little did I realise for the moment what I was playing.........Five foot two, Eyes of blue, Coogie coogie coogie coo... HAS ANYBODY SEEN MY GAL?.....In the middle of this outragious arrangement, there was Swami playing a tremendous joke on me! Not only did I have to play this line once, it came about 8 times! Imagine sitting in the middle of the packed Mandir with thousands of ladies, playing that......and it being true! I had been so concentrating on the implication of the first line we had not looked further. Swami carried on smiling....15 all!

The college boys followed us with some Hindu songs and the physics master stood up to play some brilliant piano accordian passages between verses.

90

After the second verse, everyone burst out laughing with love, including Swami, because, as the physics master started to play, at about the third open-up the accordian........suddenly fell into two pieces! Both He and we could only see the funny side.....innocent humour.

So.......HAS ANYBODY SEEN MY GAL?

ENGAGED?

After Christmas Swami called Maynard and I for an interview and, waving His right hand in the air, produced for us a beautiful gold Seiko watch each. One with a black dial for me (to match my black "tails") and one with a white dial for Maynard (who had worn white). Then in front of Maynard, He told me that I should go and choose a wife. "There are many girls from many different nationalities here, go and choose!" I said that I had gone 40 years of my life without finding one. I would only trust His judgement, not my own. Swami said that He would do everything, but I must also look. As Maynard said afterwards, I was the only man in the ashram allowed to look at ladies with Swami's permission! By now it seemed that everyone in the ashram had heard that there might be a wedding and were trying to match me up. That evening I met a very lovely Australian lady. In fact everyone had narrowed the choice down to her (unbeknown to us). The next morning I asked Swami about her and He said that I should go and ask, so..... I went and asked her about marriage. She agreed, subject to Swami being happy and giving it His blessing. In the afternoon Swami called me in again with Maynard and wanted to know the details. I told Him her name and He went off into His "computer mode", as I call it, and said that she was a very good girl. Then He seemed to look into the future and see

some problems, not with her, but with the circumstances that would arise, and so He said "No, Wait".

Imagine how I felt now having to go back to her
and saying that Swami had advised to wait!! I am sure
anywhere else in the world this would have caused a
scene, but, luckily, she had said only if Swami
agreed, so in many ways she understood.

Swami then called me in again and said that I was
now free, free to do as I wished; did I really want this
marriage, if so, He would do everything. I had
decided to offer my life to God, and for it to be used
in any way He wanted and if this marriage would
hinder this, then, NO, I did not want it at all. So I said
this. "Good" said Swami, "Now leave everything to
Swami". The next day He saw the lady and explained
things to her,which I believe helped her understand.

More and more love seemed to pour from Swami;
again He called me in, took me into the inner room
and dissolved me into tears for most of the day, not so
much with what He said, but with that overwhelming
love energy that flows through Him. He said simply,
"Your marriage is my responsibility". The reality of
what He was saying was so marvellous.

So, I wait..............

SWAMI, THE TRAVEL AGENT
AND SPORTS DAY

My return ticket showed a confirmed seat on the flight from Bombay to London on January 11th. This was the only date available when I had booked in London. Swami told me that I should stay for Sports day on 11th and to help the Bandboys with some new marches.

I tried by various contacts to change my ticket, but every agent came back with the same reply from British Airways "All flights were fully booked until January 22nd", and there was a "waiting list of at least 40 to 50 people for each flight". It seemed a hopeless situation and it was not really possible to stay until the 22nd as there were hints of work back in England. Come January 9th, I had still not been able to change the flight, so I thought that the only other possibility was to ask Swami. He came past, so I asked Him to help as I had not as yet been able to change the ticket from the 11th. He looked at me and said "You will travel on the 14th on the midnight flight from Bombay, and to get to Bombay you will take the 1300 flight from Bangalore on the 13th. Go and get your tickets and give them to me. I will also send car to take you to Bangalore."

I went and got my tickets and gave them to the man who organises Swami's travel arrangements. He

94

was as mystified as I was, because he knew that he could change internal flights, but not international. What was Swami doing? He went and telephoned British Airways, who told him exactly the same story as before, no chance as there were 40 to 50 people on the waiting list. They then asked for my name , and on checking the computer I was already on the confirmed list for the 14th!!!!!!!!

When he told me this I also mentioned to him that Swami had promised me a car, to which he replied that he was sorry, but Swami had not told him and he could not do anything without Swami's instruction. I knew that Swami had organized a taxi for Maynard and his wife on the 13th in the afternoon, but that was no use to me as I had to be in Bangalore by midday, and it is a three and a half hour drive.

I could relax as my ticket had been changed, and I could now look forward to Sports day. Maynard and I had taught the Bandboys some new marches, Liberty Bell, the RAF march and many more. So they had a good dozen marches to play for the marchpast of the students.

The day came and started at 7 a.m. at the stadium. Thousands of people were there from overseas visitors to the parents of the students. The Band was to start the proceedings playing a slow march (in 3-beats to a bar!!!) leading Swami in on his chariot. In

95

front of the procession was Sai Gita, His pet elephant, highly decorated and seemingly very happy. I was wearing my tails again as I was to conduct the Band once it had arrived by the V.I.P. stand, and Maynard was going to add some power to the trumpet section to save the Bandboys getting too tired playing for such a long time without a break.

It was a beautiful morning and everyone was seated, except Maynard and myself who were standing near the V.I.P. stand. I was about 4 metres away from the tarmac single track that went right around the stadium. Between me and the roadway sat about 3 rows of sevadals dressed in their white suits. Try to picture the scene, because those readers with a vivid imagination and a great sense of humour will appreciate fully what I went through in the five minutes that followed. With my particular sense of fun, I ended up with tears running down my face, shaking like a jelly with uncontrollable hysterical laughter. I know it was a real Swami joke judging by His smile as He went past me just after the "incident".

Sai Gita was led round and they stopped her just by me on the track. Suddenly, and totally unexpected by (me not being used to elephants in England on solemn occasions), she decided to "spend a penny". She must have been bursting, as gallons and gallons poured forth. I began to see the funny side, and Maynard standing next to me realised that I had got the giggles, so began making wickedly funny remarks in my left ear deliberately to make things worse. If only they had taken her on to the sand it would not have been so funny, but the fact that she was standing on the tarmac meant that it sprayed everywhere as it hit the ground. Maynard then whispered "Look out, her tail is going up!" She manoeuvered herself so that I had an excellent view and started....well...there was enough for father's rose garden and more! The more I tried desperately *not* to look, the more I heard, and since the ground was already very wet........I leave the rest to the imagination! Maynard whispered, "It's just as well elephants don't fly!" I'm afraid that that remark was just too much, I was now crying with laughter. At last they moved Sai Gita off onto the sand, leaving behind not only a steaming mess, but also a collection of suddenly most interestingly decorated spectators who would, no doubt, make *very* sure they never again sat on the front row!. I looked up and nearly died as the Bandboys were now approaching playing their instruments, with only socks on their feet. Their eyes said it all as they approached the scene and realised that they had no choice but to march straight through it!

There is an old show business saying "Never work with animals or children!"

Swami arrived and gave me an old fashioned smile.......The day was very entertaining with the boys and girls performing many different stunts. My heart was stolen by the little ones from the Primary School in the afternoon, they were great. A lovely day was spent with Swami and his students.

The afternoon of Friday 12th soon came round, Swami gave Darshan as usual and walked past me. As He did so I knelt up and asked whether I could speak to Him before I left the following day. "Yes" He said, "I will talk tomorrow, and the car will come to take you to Bangalore."

Again after Darshan I told His travel organiser that Swami had repeated that He would send a car for me. Again He politely pointed out that He could do nothing as Swami had not spoken to him about it. What was I to do? I decided for safety's sake I would book my own taxi for 8 a.m.

The time of Darshan had been changed to 7.45 a.m. one hour later than usual, so I wondered how He could see me and I could still get my taxi at 8 a.m. I woke early the next morning, and decided to go down early to the Mandir just in case Swami came out before time. Needless to say, He came out soon after 7 a.m. to everyone's surprise. Two government officials were there on the verandah with their security people, so again my monkey mind wondered what was going to happen. Swami called them in and then looked at Maynard and me and said "Come Pakoda 1 and Pakoda 2".

Swami saw us and told me, amongst various personal things, that I should come back again in April or May ....with wife!!!!!!!!

I asked Him about this book and whether He was happy with what I was writing, to which He said He was very happy with it and I should finish it and bring it back for Him to Bless. As time has passed I have been asked many times to recount my experiences with Swami and, although I've felt very happy in doing this, I had never had the opportunity to ask his prior permission or advice, so now seemed to be the chance. "Swami, when I return to England, may I be a messenger of your Love?" "Yes" He said, smiling."Very Happy, and I will be your messenger too!"

What did He mean????????? ah well, time will tell.

As I left He said "Car will come at 9 a. m." I went back to the flat and waited. At 8.55 two Bandboys came running up to tell me that Swami was sending a car in a few minutes.I now had confidence (!!!!!!!!) to send the hired car away at a cost of 100 rupees (£2).To my astonishment Swami, himself, sent one of His own small cars and His own driver to take me to

Bangalore.... what a typical loving surprise. We arrived at the airport at 12.40 for the 1300 flight to discover that it was half an hour late. I should have guessed it would be.When I arrived in Bombay airport, an elderly man came straight up to me and said "Sir, you are catching the midnight flight to London, I have a comfortable hotel room very cheaply, you have seven hours to wait for your flight, please come". I did not think the situation was anything out of the ordinary, but the room turned out to be very comfortable, and was rather a "God - send"?

When I arrived at the international terminal at 10 p.m. to check in for the flight to London, there were about 300 people queuing at the B.A. desks. As I walked through the door a British Airways man came up to me and said, please would I follow him, which I did to the Club class desk. I pointed out to him that I was only economy class. He said he knew that, but he wanted to check me in and send me through to the lounge so that I was not kept waiting. He checked me in and then walked away again, leaving me completely bemused as to what was really happening.

I spent the rest of the journey home going through the trip all over again in my mind, and seriously wondering how I could do my best for Swami in being a "Messenger of His Love."

MESSENGER OF LOVE

I have tried in my way to explain the experiences that I have had through my life, leading to the meeting with Sai Baba, and what has happened since then in such a short time. Reading what I have written, some readers, at the use of the words "Lord", or "God", may inwardly say "Ouch", "that's gone a bit far" or even "Blasphemy". I have not written this to offend anyone, only to give an honest picture of what is really happening a few thousand miles away in India, and, as a result of which, all around the world.

This has been the most marvellous experience of my life, which I hope every reader will share.

A good friend of mine arrived at Puttaparthi, and in the opening conversation said "I hope you don't expect me to think that Swami is God , do you!" I do not expect anyone to just accept any thoughts like that. What you can do is to look at the FACTS and not beliefs or hearsay, and make your own mind up. In fact it will be your heart that will tell you.

Just for a moment, let's look at a few of the FACTS that no-one can deny.

Through His guidance and example, Swami has masterminded the construction of many schools, colleges and the university, giving top quality

101

education, free of charge, to thousands of children each year.

Two general hospitals, one at Puttaparthi, and the other at Bangalore, treating hundreds of people every day, free.

The "Super Speciality Hospital", the second largest in Asia to which doctors and surgeons come from all over the world , and give their time doing major operations daily. This is again free of charge to anyone in the world.

He has created two major Ashrams, one at Puttaparthi, and one at Whitefield near Bangalore.

He is continually doing good, helping people, advising them from all walks of life. Everyday, He comes to give His Blessing, or Darshan, twice. Once in the morning, and once in the afternoon. He does not accept money Himself, although there are some strictly controlled Trusts to which one can make a donation to help pay for the medicines used at the hospitals, for example.

He does not want you to "sign up" to Him, or set up a new religion. His message is LOVE, and He says if you are a Christian (for example), go back to your country and be a better Christian.

These are facts, and I cannot find anything wrong with them so far. All these things we can relate to in our everyday life, so perhaps He is just a very great man?

Now I would like to mention again some of the things that I have seen, but cannot understand in terms of my everyday life. He waves His hand in a circular manner and ash called Vibhuti falls from it. What is the point of this, one wonders, until you discover that it is used as a medicine and has apparently cured thousands upon thousands of people. As long as it does good there can be nothing wrong in it. Sometimes tablets are also "produced".

He also produces "gifts" for people, like the ring and watch He has given me.

Why? Well, for me it has proved the reality of what is going on. When you are sitting back at home remembering all the incredible things you have experienced, then to be able to *hold* something confirms to your "monkey mind" that your experience was not a dream. I know some people feel that there are so many poor people, why not help them.......but He does in every constructive way possible. He has provided homes, sewing machines, tractors, water supplies, special wheelchairs for the severely handicapped...... and the list is limitless...none of which I needed for my life and understanding. Think of these rings and things as more of an anchor, an anchor to the reality of "God's work" that is going on in the world today. I am equally certain that each of these "gifts" does, or will, have a special significance to the person He gives them to......only time will tell.

There are photographs from all round the world with Him "appearing" on them. I accept that you may think that they are fakes, well perhaps.......but all of them?

I have seen (and there are countless recorded incidents) of Him touching critically ill people in wheelchairs, with cancer etc., and they are healed. These people have come from all over the world, so to have "set the whole thing up" is rather out of the question. Yes, I know some folk say " mind over matter". Does it matter? The important thing surely is that the person got better. People never have this sceptical attitude when they read the stories of Jesus.

He has, as He has proved to me on a very personal level, knowledge of everything that you have done and do, and can give the most loving advice.

How can you explain this incredible energy, which fills you, warms you, and surrounds you with the most fantastic feeling of being part of Love? Bliss is the word He uses. One day I know YOU will feel this and I know you will understand then why it is so impossible for me, or anyone else, to put this into words. You will *never* forget the feeling for the rest of your life.

There is no other "Man" in the world today like Swami. As He says, "My life is my message". Some friends have said, why doesn't He just wave His hand and put the world to right?........How *long* would it last "right" if He did? Mankind must *change* and follow the message from all the great Masters, Teachers, Avatars, use what title you like, and that message is so SIMPLE. It is the message of LOVE.

Coming back to England, to a staff room where "Bailey's trips to India" have caused untold mirth, has kept my feet firmly on the ground when reflecting on what has happened, and it does not change one second of it!

There are many books of stories over the past 40 years about Swami, read them, make up your own mind. Two thousand years ago Jesus lived, and we in the western world have been brought up following the stories of His life and teachings. I do not want to enter into an argument taking odd sentences out of the Bible to make my points as I love and respect the Bible passages. I can find nothing in the life and teachings of Sai Baba that does anything but bring the Bible (and all the other great traditional religious scripts from around the world) to life, and brings God's message to a very practical use in the modern world.

I know that some will say that, as a starting point, He is the greatest Holy Man on earth today. Surely, what matters is that we all try to change the world for the better NOW, and not argue as to whether someone who is putting the fantastic message into practice is "God" or not. We need to follow His example in our own lives. Each one of us has our own concept and acceptance of who "God" is, was, should be, or is not, so let's leave that for our hearts to decide. What we <u>can</u> do is to unite our thoughts into making this world a more loving, caring, beautiful place for everyone and everything.

We no longer have to believe...... LOOK OVER THERE......, you can see for yourself. HE is the JOY and the LIGHT OF THE WORLD............you can now <u>KNOW</u>.

THOUGHTS AND SUGGESTIONS

Many friends have listened to my experiences, some have been and seen for themselves, some have borrowed books and videos which have convinced them that Sai Baba is a very great man. Some have gone further, but everyone has said in their way "What can I do.......or do I do...... now?"

My thoughts and suggestions are these. Swami is the Greatest Friend that you will ever have in your life, so treat Him as one. Talk to Him wherever you are, either out loud or in your head. Never be afraid to ask Him, or talk to Him about anything, even the most trivial things, discuss them with Him.

He is Real and is Everywhere all the time, so He knows every moment of your life. You cannot hide anything from Him, so why try to? Talk to Him about your problems, desires, He will help you. If you want to stop smoking, for example, and you genuinely want to, ask Him to help you. I am sure you will be amazed at the help you get in many ways. He can do anything, but He will only help when you call Him.

If you find it difficult at the moment to speak to Him in your mind, then don't be afraid to write to Him. Ask Him simply, and to the point, to show you which way to go, or to help in whatever the situation may be. You must remember that He loves you and will only react in a loving way.

Sometimes I have looked at someone who is ill and wished that I could help them in some way. In reality we do not know the real reason for their condition, and we have no right to interfere with someone else's life. I have found however, that by asking Swami to be with that person and imagining them covered in the most beautiful white or golden light (in my mind coming from Swami) often circumstances alter around them, and as a result they begin to think about life. This is often the beginning of a lasting process of change within them.

So if He is real, and knows all about you, why does He let you have all the problems and sometimes disasters in your life? I know, looking back at my life so far, that all the things that I thought were disasters at the time were not, and I would not have missed going through them for anything.

If you get the chance to go and see Swami, and it will be quite clear when this moment arrives, then I suggest that you prepare yourself before you go . Spend a few moments each morning and evening, perhaps sitting in your favourite chair, and ask him in your mind to make you aware of what might happen. From my experience and listening to other people, once you are there the very least you will experience is the very different energy that is there. What does this energy do for you?

Swami lives in India and as a result is surrounded by the Hindu religion, but please remember that Swami stands for all religions or none, and I am sure that if He had been born in England, for example, He would have been surrounded by the Christian church. Do not under any circumstances think that to get close to Swami you have to become Hindu, or anything else. Everyone can go to Swami directly, your heart to His heart, just give Him your love, that is all He wants of us.

Another friend came to see me one evening and said, "David, this may sound silly, but I've never really bothered about going to church, or praying, in fact I'm not sure that I know how to. Somehow I feel that I can relate to the work that Swami is doing and I would like to help in some way. What can I do? How do I start? Can I really talk to Him here, and can He hear me thousands of miles away? What do I say?"

Well, why not do what I did, just be honest and open about how you feel, and tell Him. Try this....for example.....sit quietly in your favourite chair, and, with no-one else around, and talk quietly to Him, as though He is sitting next to you, and say this perhaps?

"Swami, I am sitting here in my chair feeling somewhat foolish. I've never thought of a real "God" before, let alone talking to Him. To be honest I'm not sure, even now. I've heard about YOU, read about YOU and within me I would really like to talk to YOU and ask for YOUR help........but how?

Swami, YOU, I am told, know everything about me. I find that difficult to understand, but anyhow, I have my own problems........please help. Please show me in YOUR way that YOU are there and are helping. I know that the answers and solutions I may get may not be the results I am expecting, but in a funny way I do think that YOU will only do what is best for me........after all, that is what I would really want anyway.

Swami, please send this love of YOURS that everyone talks about, into my life. Protect my family. It would be great to feel that through all the trouble and problems in the world that we live in, YOU can, and do things for the good. Please help me to experience YOUR work, because inside me I, too, only want lovely things to happen. I have many frustrations which really distress me...... please keep me calm and stop me worrying.

Swami, I want to know YOU, and be able to trust YOU........please help."

Some other thoughts that I find helpful in day to day life are these:

"Swami, when I am about to say something sharply to someone, teach me to remember to think ..... would Swami say that?

Swami, when I am about to do something in retaliation to someone, teach me to remember to think.....would Swami do that?

Swami, when I am working and want to do a quick job, teach me to remember to think.....would Swami do the job like that?

Swami, when I am about to do something that I really know is wrong, teach me to remember to think.......would Swami do that?

Swami, please teach me to remember that You are always there, so that when I am fed up, frustrated, angry, I can always "shout" at You, and not take it out on others, who often have their own problems. In Your love You have promised that I can give You all my anxieties, worries, and You will help.

Teach me to remember that You are in everything, so You are the person I was going to be rude to, hurt, offend, and You are the person that I was about to think didn't care about me.

Swami, I'm sorry, please forgive me and be with me. Help me to feel Your presence, with all Your love.....now......Lord please.......teach me to understand.

At the beginning of the day why not say something like.......

Another day is starting, Swami,
Please be with me, guide my thoughts
    throughout the day.
Help me to think before I speak, so that I
    do not hurt anyone today.
Please make me a stronger channel of
    Your love and light.
Take my life today, Swami, let every breath
    be for You and full of Your love
Let every deed I do be in Your name.

At the end of the day, why not try............

Swami, another day ends, and many times
    today I have forgotten you, yet
I know You have not forgotten me.
Thoughtless moments and actions have
    happened today.
Please forgive me, and help me to forgive
    all those who have annoyed me today.

Help me to see things from their point of view. Teach me to do things as I would always want to do them for You.

Never be afraid of making up your own thoughts, requests or "prayers" on any subject about which you feel concern, such as.....

People in hospital.....those at home seriously ill........animals.....the homeless...... alcoholics......... bringing peace to the world........nature...........rain forests ......oceans.......the world itself........the bereaved ....leaders of the nations.........your family......... understanding...........etc.

We all live in a world that is in turmoil, and we all need to stop and think of what the consequences might be if we carry on abusing the wonderful life that we have each been given. It is not too late, that is one of the reasons why Sai Baba is here now, to show us the way in the modern world, and to guide each and every one of us towards a lifetime engulfed in the love of God.

THERE'S ONLY ONE
LOVE

Words and Music by David Bailey

There's only one love,
The love I adore,
That love comes from you dear Lord,
Please love me evermore.

vs: Wintertime and Summertime
        Springtime and Fall,
        Everyday in every way
        Your love transends it all

There's ....

vs: Sometimes Lord we stray away,
        Thinking not of you, yet,
        Everyday in every way
        you guide us back to you.

There's ....

Thank you Lord for everything
that you've come to do.
Teach us Lord to follow thee,
Our lives we give to you.

There's ....

Sathya Sai, oh Sathya Sai,
Please forgive us Lord,
Give us Lord the power to be
Your servants one and all.

115

REFLECTIONS

Here are some of my favourite "reflections" to muse over in a quiet minute or two.....or three?

THERE IS ONLY ONE RACE,
THE RACE OF HUMANITY.
THERE IS ONLY ONE LANGUAGE,
THE LANGUAGE OF THE HEART.
THERE IS ONLY ONE RELIGION,
THE RELIGION OF LOVE.
THERE IS ONLY ONE GOD,
HE IS OMNIPRESENT.

SAI BABA.

When the wind blows, the clouds rush across the sky
The wild rain pours down feeding natures needs
.................But Why?................
This earth with its moods of Sun to snow,
gives her shell on which to live.
Mankind so carefully responds to her love by ravaging
her beauty within and without.
Her lovely rain forests scream with pain of acid rain
The caverns that were full of nature's oil
now echo, void, of years of nature's toil.
.... But Why?..............
Man's greed for you and me cares not for that loving
force of life, which, if only he thought, feeds him with
food with which to live.
So think, now, not then, when time has passed, and all
is ruined, just for gain, for him, or her, who has now
left this plane for higher realms, where they now know,
and understand the carnage they have left behind for us,
.........for us.........for us to try and repair.
So stop, now, think, and act, give that love that you
have to Mother earth, as she can only give all her love
to you, unceasing and unending, whilst trying to restore
her beauty for all............

Anon.

Life is a challenge, meet it!..............
Life is a dream, realise it!
Life is a game, play it!..............
Life is love............enjoy it!

... *Sai Baba.*

118

I know, I wouldn't,
shouldn't, couldn't then
let's face it she was an old hag,
always moaning, always being hard done by.
Yet, why did I go? Why did I try to care?
There was something....what was it?
an old lady sitting there in her chair,
at war with the world, her health, her life
yet, she had made someone a fantastic wife.
Now in her last wiser years, something calls to me
from inside where I cannot see.
I feel it in me that somehow I know her
from years ago, perhaps a lifetime before.
Yes, I remember that glimpse of the past flashes
through my mind, come on memory, unwind.
Recall those moments, some centuries ago
when it was I, yes I remember
the old haggard woman, who drank,
stank, and shouted about.
That young child who always helped me back
to my shack in the woods.
I remember the love in her face, yes, when you
looked in her eyes they seemed to go on for ever.
they twinkled with joy as I helped then.
So life's round about has come round again,
that's what I see in reverse this time, that's why
I love her.
She is that love that transcends all time
It's in you and in me.........

So find it, and share it.......it's love and it's free.

Anon.

119

Truth is within ourselves; it takes no rise
From outward things, what'er you may believe.
There is an inmost centre in us all,
Where truth abides in fullness.

Browning.

What a piece of work is man!
How noble in reason
How infinite in faculty
In apprehension how like a God.

Hamlet.

I know not where His islands lift
Their fronded palms in air.
I only know I cannot drift
Beyond His love and care.

Whittier.

Are you in earnest? Seize this very minute:
What can you do, or dream you can, begin it;
Boldness has genius, power, and magic in it
Only engage, and then the mind grows heated;
Begin, and then the work will be completed.

Goethe.

120

Let there be many windows in your soul,
That all the glory of the universe
May beauty in it. Not a narrow pane
Of one poor creed can catch the radiant rays
 That shine from countless sources. Tear away
The blinds of superstition; let light
Pour through fair windows, broad as truth itself
And high as heaven.....Tune your ear
To all the worldless music of the stars
And to the voice of nature, and your heart
Shall turn to truth and goodness as the plant
Turns to the sun. A thousand unseen hands
Reach down to help you to their peace
crowned heights
And all the forces of the firmament
Shall fortify your strength. Be not afraid
To thrust aside half-truths and grasp the whole.

Anon.

I dreamed that stone by stone I reared a sacred fane, a Temple, neither pagoda, mosque, nor church, but loftier, simpler, always open-doored to every breath from heaven, and Truth and Peace and Love and Justice came and dwelt therein. *Tennyson.*

In the beginning was the Word, and the Word was with God, and the Word was God. The same was in the beginning with God. All things were made by Him; and without Him was not anything made that was made. In Him was life; and the life was the light of men.

St John ch 1 vs1-4.

121

Lord,

Make me an instrument of Thy peace.
Where there is hatred let me sow love.
Where there is injury, pardon;
Where there is doubt, faith;
Where there is despair, hope;
Where there is darkness, light; and
Where there is sadness, joy.

O Divine Master,

Grant that I may not so much
Seek to be consoled as to console;
To be understood as to understand;
To be loved as to love.
For it is in giving we receive,
It is in pardoning that we are pardoned, and
It is in dying that we are born to eternal life.

St Francis of Assisi.

Your daily life is your Temple and your religion
Whenever you enter into it take with you your all.
Take the plough and the forge and the mallet and the
     lute,
The things you have fashioned in necessity or for delight.
For in reverie you cannot rise above your achievements
     nor fall below your failures.
And take with you all men:
For in adoration you cannot fly higher than their hopes
     nor humble yourself lower than their despair.
             ******

And if you would know God, be not therefore a solver of
     riddles.
Rather look about you and you shall see Him playing
     with our children.
And look into space; you shall see Him in the cloud Out-
     stretching His arms walking in the lightening and
     descending rain.
You shall see Him Smiling in the flowers,
Then rising and waving His hands in trees.
            ****

Love gives naught but itself and takes naught but from
     itself.
Love possesses not nor would it be possessed;
For love is sufficient unto love.
            ****

When you love you should not say "God is in my
     heart," but rather "I am in the heart of God."
And think not you can direct the course of love, for love,
     if it finds you worthy, directs your course.
       Excerpts from The Prophet. By Kahlil Gibran.
            123

"SEEKE OUT YE GOODE IN EVERIE MAN, AND SPEKE OF ALLE THE BEST YE CAN."

Chaucer

I had rather be a door keeper in the house of my God, than to dwell in the tents of wickedness.

Psalm 84 verse 10

It is better to trust in the Lord than to put confidence in man.

Psalm 118 verse 8

The Lord shall preserve thy going out and thy coming in from this time forth and for evermore.

Psalm 121 verse 8

God be in my head, and in my understanding;
God be in my eyes, and in my looking;
God be in my mouth, and in my speaking;
God be in my heart, and in my thinking;
God be at my end , and at my departing.

Teach me my God and King,
In all things thee to see
And what I do in anything
To do it as for thee.

George Herbert.

Lord, we thy presence seek,
May ours this blessing be,
Give us a pure and lowly heart
A temple meet for thee.

Keble.

THE LOTUS FEET

BABA WITH SAI GEETHA

SWAMI

WATCHING NEW YEARS PERFORMANCE

OUR LORD SAI

DHARSAN ON CHRISTMAS DAY

                         DHARSAN FROM THE CHARIOT

SWAMI AND HIS "GREATEST DEVOTEE"

SWAMI AT KODAIKANAL

"Whatever road I take joins the highway that leads to
   thee,"
   says the inspired writer from the Persian scriptures.

"Broad is the carpet God has spread, and beautiful the
   colours He has given it."
"The pure man respects every form of faith."
   says the Buddhist.

"My doctrine makes no difference between high and
   low, rich and poor; like the sky it has room for all,
   and like the water, it washes all alike."
"The broad-minded see the truth in different religions; the narrow-minded see only the differences."
   says the Chinese.

"The narrow minded ask,"Is this man a stranger, or is
   he of our tribe?" But to those in whom love dwells,
   the whole world is but one family."
   says the Hindu.

"Altar flowers are of many species, but all worship
    is one."
"Heaven is a palace with many doors, and each may
    enter in his own way."
"Are we not all children of one Father?
                        says the Christian.

"That which was profitable to the soul of man the
    Father revealed to the ancients;
That which is profitable to the soul of man to-day
    revealeth He this day."
                    says the Later-day seer.

If   the   earth
were   only   a   few   feet   in
diameter, floating a few feet above
a field somewhere, people would come
from everywhere to marvel at it. People would
walk   around it marvelling at its big pools of
water, its little pools and the water flowing between
the pools. People would marvel at the bumps on it,
and the holes in it, and they would marvel at the very
thin layer of gas surrounding it and the water suspended
in the gas. The people would marvel at all the creatures
walking around the surface of the ball, and at the creatures
in the water. The people would declare it was precious
because it was the only one and they would protect
it so that it would not be hurt. The ball would be the
greatest wonder known and people would come to behold
it, to be healed, to gain knowledge, to know beauty
and to wonder how it could be. People would love
it,   and   defend it with   their lives because
they would somehow know that their lives,
their own roundness, could be nothing
without   it. If the earth   were
only   a   few   feet   in
d i a m e t e r.

Anon.

127

Prayer is not asking,
It is a longing of the soul.
It is a daily admission
of ones weakness.
It is better in prayer
to have a heart without
words, than words without
a heart

Gandhi.

Perfect love makes no demands,
and seeks nothing for itself.

*****

There is no such thing as
right or wrong love, since
for it to be love at all,
the other's happiness comes
first.

Sister Wendy Beckett.

"Come unto me all ye that are heavy laden, and I will
give you rest."

Matthew ch.11, vs.28.

From Love comes the beginning,
From the beginning comes questions,
From questions come answers,
From answers comes learning,
From learning comes knowledge,
From knowledge comes understanding,
From understanding comes wisdom,
From wisdom comes Love.

Graham Bishop.

If you want peace,
and if you want happiness
you must live in love.
Only through love will you find inner peace.
Only through love will you find true happiness.
Love flourishes through giving and forgiving.
Develop your love.
Immerse yourself in love.
Love knows no hatred,
Love is free from all selfishness,
Love is far removed from anger.
Love never takes, it only gives.
......LOVE IS GOD.......

Sai Baba.

Suggested Reading :-

A Catholic Priest Meets Sai Baba
           by Don Mario Mazzoleni

Sai Baba The Holy Man and Psychiatrist
           by Dr.Samuel H. Sandweiss

Sathya Sai Baba The Embodiment of Love
           by Peggy Mason & Ron Laing

DAVID'S CASSETTES

Pure Gold - Blessed by Swami including Warsaw Concerto, Strauss Moonlight Sonata, Claire De Lune, Pachebel Canon-Mozart-Satie and many more timeless classics.

Your Favourite Melodies - This includes my special arrangement of Phantom of the Opera and Oklahoma, Charlie Kunz, Exmoor Rhapsody etc.

Golden Piano Favourites - This is perhaps the most popular selection (especially in the car!) including the Rapsodie Les 2 Caps that I wrote and Glenn Miller, French Medley, Stardust, Love Story, Laras Theme, lots to hum along to.

Music Maestro Please - More of a Sing-a-Long selection from Flanagan & Allan, Ivor Novello, Sound of Music, Danny Boy.

Golden Musical Memories - A lovely selection from the wartime years, The Entertainer, Me & My Girl, Memory from Cats and many more.

The Golden Touch of David Bailey - Lots of melodies from My Fair Lady, Irving Berlin, As Time Goes By and many more.

Music to Dream By - Gentle "inspired" music at the Piano. If you want music for relaxation or Healing to then this is for you. This is extensively used in Healing Centres & Hospitals.

Cassettes £6 + £1 pfp. Mail your orders along with your payment to Mr. David Bailey by Bank draft payable at England.

BOOK REVIEWS

☆ *Good Chances by Howard Levin.*

Published by Sri Sathya Sai Towers Hotels Pvt. Ltd., 3/497,
Main Road, Prasanthi Nilayam - 515 134, Rs.120/-.

ॐ ॐ ॐ

Good Chances by Howard Levin is an autobiographical
account of the author's quest in the early phase of his life.
In 11 chapters, he records how he came under the divine
influence of Bhagavan Sri Sathya Sai Baba in the early
1970's -- as Elsie I. Cowan rightly puts it, "A relaxed,
quiet period at Brindavan and Prasanthi Nilayam when a
group of young westerners had the opportunity to live,
work and receive spiritual guidance from the Avatar of
this age."

The author was a student at Arizona State University
in the college of architecture. To find freedom and realize
his true self, he set out on a quest. He travelled through
England, France, Italy, Yugoslavia, Greece and Turkey.

India and Marsha, who he had met early at Istanbul,
had since been crossing him in his travels off and on.
They wrote to him about their stay at Sri Sai Baba's ashram
at Whitefield, and they wished him to join them. So on
June 5, 1970 Howard reached Whitefiled. There he settled
along with the nineteen other westerners, and began a
career of acquaintances with Bhagavan Sri Sathya Sai Baba.
He was one of the fortunate few on whom Swami bestowed
personal attention, and found time to visit them in their
work and leisure and talk to them on spiritual and mundane
affairs. They were more than convinced that He was their
loving, approving mother, their friend, well-wisher and
guide. They were equally thrilled at the glimpses of His
divinity he privileged them with now and then.

The author has found his God in Human form. The
truth of His Being ever fills his heart with joy. His life
has been redeemed from the aimless drift that characterizes
every modern youth.

It is a good chance to read this book. The author has
succeeded in capturing the speech rhythms of Bhagavan
Baba. The incantatory cadences of Bhagavan Baba in the
book render its reading a spiritual sadhana and a permanent
solace.

☆ Sathya Sai's Amrita Varshini by Sudha Aditya

Published by Sri Sathya Sai Towers Hotels Pvt. Ltd., 3/497
Main Road, Prasanthi Nilayam-515 134, India. pp.77, Rs.75/-.

***

Bhagavan Baba's teachings are like nectar showers, drenching the inner spirit with love and bliss. The author received divine messages during her dhyana sessions. He guided her through the Inner Voice. He gave her elucidations on life, truth and spiritualism. When she prayed intensely to Bhagavan he confirmed the authenticity of the messages in a Dream Darshan.

She was lucky to keep a record of them. Now she presents the messages in the form of conversations with Bhagavan Baba, in response to His Divine Command to share them with fellow devotees. The compilation is arranged in ten chapters providing clarifications on ordinary spiritual exercises like Sathwic Food and Fasting to profound spiritual truths of Incarnation and Karmic Law.

Swami once explained to her the greatness of silence. When the mind is silent, the voice of God can be heard. So practise mauna as a discipline. When the tongue is quiet, the ears are unresponsive and the mind is not affected by external factors, the mind becomes calm and you will experience a sense of deep peace within yourself. When the mind is silent you will have extra energy to think and work better.

Faith and confidence in God are inevitable concomitants that would act as a catalyst in the functioning of God's will and ushering in a new era. Faith refers to His Omnipresent, Omnipotent and Omniscient nature. Confidence refers to trust in His Word, Will and Work.

The basic criteria regarding food are its right quality and quantity. One eats to live, not lives to eat. Along with food the basic discipline of speak no evil, see no evil, hear no evil and do no evil should be practised. Fasting in Sanskrit is Upavasa; which means living near God. A disciplined life is the surest way to reach us near God.

Swami explains the purpose of incarnation in memorable words. God always incarnates to demonstrate the unity of all religions and faiths and to establish a common brotherhood of man and Fatherhood of God. Miracles are his visiting cards. He uses them to attract people towards the Godward path. Once their faith is established, they begin to receive from God what he has really come to give - Knowledge and Bliss.

The book reads as the quintessential Sai teachings.

OUR PUBLICATIONS

01. 70 QS & AS. ON PRACTICAL SPIRITUALITY
    AND SATHYA SAI BABA   - O.P.Vidyakar   Rs. 90
02. A JOURNEY TO LOVE (Fourth Edition)   - David Bailey   Rs.180
03. "ALEX" THE DOLPHIN   - Johnima Wintergate   Rs. 90
04. A STORY OF INDIA AND
    PATAL BHUVANESWAR   - Jennifer Warren   Rs. 60
05. A COMPENDIUM OF THE TEACHINGS OF
    SATHYA SAI BABA (Second Edition)   - Charlene Leslie-Chadan Rs.555
06. ASHES,ASHES WE ALL FALL DOWN   - Gloria St. John   Rs. 80
07. BAPU TO BABA   - V.K. Narasimhan   Rs.120
08. BHAGAVAN SRI SATHYA SAI BABA
    DISCOURSES IN KODAIKANAL, APRIL 96 - Pooja Kapahi   Rs.120
09. BUDO-KA-TRUE SPIRITUAL WARRIORS   - Deena Naidu   Rs.200
10. CRICKET FOR LOVE
    A Souvenir on Sri Sathya Sai Unity Cup   Rs.250
11. CUTTING THE TIES   - Phyllis Krystal   Rs.110
12. CUTTING MORE TIES THAT BIND   - Phyllis Krystal   Rs.120
13. CUTTING THE TIES - WORK BOOK   - Phyllis Krystal   Rs.140
14. DA PUTTAPARTHI
    A PATAL BHUVANESHWAR (Italian)   - Sandra Percy   Rs.150
15. DEATHING (Indian Edition)   - Anya Foos-Graber   Rs.195
16. DISCOVERING MARTIAL ARTS   - Deena Naidu   Rs.265
17. DIVINE LEELAS OF BHAGAVAN
    SRI SATHYA SAI BABA   - Nagamani Purnaiya   Rs. 90
18. EDUCATION IN HUMAN VALUES
    (3 Vols.) (Indian Edition)   - June Auton   Rs.750
19. GLIMPSES OF THE DIVINE   - Birgitte Rodriguez   Rs.150
20. GOOD CHANCES (Second Edition)   - Howard Levin   Rs.120
21. GOD AND HIS GOSPEL   - Dr. M.N.Rao   Rs.120
22. GOD DESCENDS ON EARTH   - Sanjay Kant   Rs. 60
23. GOD LIVES IN INDIA   - R. K. Karanjia   Rs. 75
24. HEART TO HEART (Reprint)   - Howard Levin   Rs.120
25. IN QUEST OF GOD   - P.P. Arya   Rs.120
26. KNOW THYSELF (Second Edition)   - Gerard T. Satvic   Rs.180
27. LET ME SOW LOVE   - Doris May Gibson   Rs.120
28. LETTERS FROM A GRANDFATHER   - S. K. Bose   Rs.180
29. MESSAGES (JAPANEESE)   - Dr. M.N. Rao   Rs.150
30. MIRACLES ARE MY VISITING CARDS
    (Indian Edition)   - Erlendur Haraldsson   Rs. 180
31. MOHANA BALA SAI (Children's Book)   - Sai Mira   Rs.120
32. MUKTI THE LION FINDS HIMSELF   - Gina Suritsch   Rs. 85
33. MESSAGES FROM MY DEAREST
    FRIEND SAI BABA   - Elvie Bailey   Rs.130
34. NARA NARAYANA GUFA ASHRAM Part III - Swami Maheswaranand Rs. 20
35. PRASANTHI GUIDE   - R. Padmanaban   Rs. 50
36. SAI BABA GITA   - Al. Drucker   Rs.240
37. SAI BABA: THE ETERNAL COMPANION   - B. P. Misra   Rs.100
38. SELF REALISATION   - Al. Drucker   Rs. 35
39. SATVIC FOOD & HEALTH
    (Second Revised Edition)   - Gerard T. Satvic   Rs. 40

OUR PUBLICATIONS ...

40.SAI SANDESH	- Sai Usha	Rs. 50
41.SAI MY DIVINE BELOVED	- Sai Usha	Rs. 50
42.SATHYA SAI'S ANUGRAHA VARSHINI (Reprint)	- Sudha Aditya	Rs. 90
43.SATHYA SAI'S AMRITA VARSHINI (Second Edition)	- Sudha Aditya	Rs. 75
44.SRI SATHYA SAI CHALEESA	- B.P. Mishra	Rs. 15
45.SATVIC STORIES	- Benjamin Kurzweil	Rs. 30
46.SAI HUMOUR	- Peggy Mason & Others	Rs. 65
47.SCRIPTURES ARE FULFILLED	- Kristina Gale-Kumar	Rs.160
48.SPRINKLES OF GOLDEN DUST	- Jeannette Caruth	Rs. 65
49.SRI SATHYA SAI BABA AND WONDERS OF HIS LOVE	- John Elliott	Rs. 90
50.SONG BIRD	- LightStorm	Rs. 60
51.SRI SATHYA SAI BABA PRAYER BOOK		Rs. 10
52.SRI SATHYA SAI BABA YOUNG ADULTS PROGRAMME	- L.A. Ramdath	Rs. 80
53.SPIRITUAL IMPRESSIONS A BI-MONTHLY MAGAZINE		Rs.100
54.STUDY CIRCLES FOR DIVINITY	- Ross Woodward & Ron Farmer	Rs.390
55.THE ARMOUR OF SRI SATHYA SAI	- O. P. Vidyakar	Rs. 10
56.THE OMNIPRESENCE OF SAI	- R. Lowenberg	Rs.120
57.THE PHOENIX RETURNS	- Kristina Gale-Kumar	Rs.250
58.THE PROPHECY	- Barbara Gardner	Rs.120
59.TEN STEPS TO KESAVA	- Johnima Wintergate	Rs.150
60.THY WILL BE DONE	- C.D. Mirchandani	Rs. 90
61.WAITING FOR BABA	- V. Ramnath	Rs. 95

FORTHCOMING PUBLICATIONS ...

01.A JOURNEY TO LOVE (Spanish)	- David Bailey
02.A JOURNEY TO LOVE (Telugu)	- David Bailey
03.AT THE FEET OF SAI	- R. Lowenberg
04.DIRECTORY OF MASTERS,SAINTS, ASHRAMS AND HOLY PLACES IN INDIA	- R.Padmanaban
05.VOICE OF THE AVATAR 1994	- Sri Sathya Sai Baba
06.VOICE OF THE AVATAR 1995	- Sri Sathya Sai Baba
07.VOICE OF THE AVATAR 1996	- Sri Sathya Sai Baba
08.FACE TO FACE WITH GOD	- V.I.K. Sarin
09.FOUNTAIN OF LOVE - An Overview of Sathya Sai Water Supply Project	
10.GLORY OF SAI PADHUKAS	
11.HOLY MISSION DIVINE VISION	- Sai Usha
12.KRISHNAMURTHI AND THE FOURTH WAY	- Evan Grans
13.RAJU GOES TO SCHOOL	
14.SAI BABA AND GOLDEN LINGAM	- Murthy

15.SAI DARSHAN	- Vimla Sahni
16.SAI's STORY	- Shaila Hattiangadi
17.SAI NAMAVALI	- Jagat Narain Tripathi
18.THE ESSENTIAL REALITY	
OF ALL GOD FORMS	- O. P. Vidyakar
19.THE THOUSAND SONGS OF	
LORD VISHNU	- Jeannette Caruth
20.THE HEART OF SAI	- R. Lowenberg
21.THE GRACE OF SAI	- R. Lowenberg
22.YOGA THERAPY	- R. Lowenberg
23.SANSKRIT-ENGLISH- DICTIONARY	
24.ENGLISH BHAJANS	
25.INDIAN BHAJANS	

Books are despatched by Registered Book Post. Copies can be had by sending Money Order/International Money Order/Demand Draft drawn in favour of SRI SATHYA SAI TOWERS HOTELS PVT. LTD Payable at any Bank at Bangalore or Prasanthi Nilayam, addressed to Sai Towers, 3/497, Main Road, Prasanthi Nilayam - 515 134, India.

POSTAGE :-

India :- At the rate of 50 ps. per 100 gms. plus Rs.12/- for Registration. Maximum 5 KG. Packing and Forwarding charges per parcel is Rs.40/-

Overseas:- 5 KGS by Sea Mail to North America, South America, Europe Rs.171. Singapore, Malaysia, Australia etc. Rs.147/- plus packing and forwarding Rs.60 per parcel.

NOTE :-

*THE PRICES SHOWN ABOVE WERE CORRECT AT THE TIME OF GOING TO PRESS, IT MAY DIFFER FROM THOSE PREVIOUSLY ADVERTISED.